SETTING
LEADERSHIP
PRIORITIES

SETTING LEADERSHIP PRIORITIES

What's Necessary, What's Nice, *and* What's Got to Go

SUZETTE LOVELY

CORWIN PRESS
A SAGE Publications Company
Thousand Oaks, California

For information:

Corwin Press
A Sage Publications Company
2455 Teller Road
Thousand Oaks, California 91320
www.corwinpress.com

Sage Publications Ltd.
1 Oliver's Yard
55 City Road
London EC1Y 1SP
United Kingdom

Sage Publications India Pvt. Ltd.
B-42, Panchsheel Enclave
Post Box 4109
New Delhi 110 017 India

Printed in the United States of America

Library of Congress Cataloging-in-Publication Data

Lovely, Suzette, 1958-
Setting leadership priorities: What's necessary, what's nice, and what's got to go / Suzette Lovely.
        p. cm.
Includes bibliographical references and index.
ISBN 1-4129-1575-9 (cloth) — ISBN 1-4129-1576-7 (pbk.)
    1. School management and organization. 2. Educational leadership.
I. Title.
LB2805.L65 2006
371.2—dc22   2005014945

This book is printed on acid-free paper.

05   06   07   08   09   10   9   8   7   6   5   4   3   2   1

Acquisitions Editor:	Elizabeth Brenkus
Editorial Assistant:	Candice L. Ling
Production Editor:	Diane S. Foster
Copy Editor:	Julie Gwin
Typesetter:	C&M Digitals (P) Ltd.
Proofreader:	Cheryl Rivard
Indexer:	Molly Hall
Cover Designer:	Michael Dubowe
Graphic Designer:	Scott Van Atta

Contents

Preface

LEADERSHIP FOR ORDINARY FOLKS

Not only does leadership matter, it is second only to teaching among school-related factors influencing student achievement, according to a 2004 report commissioned by the Wallace Foundation (Leithwood, Louis, Anderson, & Wahlstrom, 2004). By setting clear direction, developing people, and creating conditions that support, rather than inhibit, teaching and learning, high-quality leaders work vicariously through others to move their organizations forward.

It is widely recognized today that educational leadership is more than 24 units of coursework and a master's degree. In the broadest sense, leadership has been described as

> the process wherein an individual member of an organization influences the interpretation of events, the choice of strategies, the [arrangement] of work activities, the motivation of people to achieve objectives, the maintenance of cooperative relationships, the development of skills and competence, and the enlistment of support from people outside the group. (Yukl, 1998, p. 5)

The question that remains is, how can contemporary leaders zero in on what is necessary, what is nice, and what has got to go?

The canvas of school leadership is painted with many names and faces. Words like *instructional, moral, participatory, servant, ethical, distributed,* and *transformational* capture the different approaches for getting the job done. Unfortunately, so many labels can take leaders off course in search of a magic formula for success. Trying to match one particular method to good leadership hides the more important themes inherent in doing what is right, irrespective of a given style or attribute. Thankfully, effective practices are now defined with empirical data to help leaders keep their eye on learning.

Educational leaders are keenly aware of the important work that must be done to provide a strong foundation for young people so that they leave high school equipped to lead productive and fulfilling lives. The difficulty lies in establishing boundaries to stay healthy and resilient in carrying out this momentous charge. One imposing obstacle comes from all the gadgetry that keeps busy executives connected to their jobs around the clock. With the cyber world taking over the workplace like a fast-moving comet, it is tough to know when we are actually on duty and when we are not. Like disposable lighters, some of us continue to burn until our flame runs out. Going unplugged now and again gives administrators the chance to catch their breath.

Whether you are a superintendent striving to visit schools regularly, a principal struggling to get into classrooms more often, or a central office manager waiting for things to slow down to take a vacation, administrators are hesitant to leave their offices because doing so parlays into additional work when they return. Adding to the dilemma is the reality that there is always some distraction that beckons people away from meaningful activities toward less important—yet seemingly urgent—matters. *Setting Leadership Priorities* is designed to provide readers with the courage and wherewithal to either (a) step back from the fray, (b) ask, "Who is better equipped to handle this problem?" or (c) say "no thank you" without feeling guilty about it. When leaders take a time-out, they invariably come back with a fresh perspective.

As ordinary folks, it is time to draw a line in the sand by simplifying more and anguishing less. Contrary to what has been said about superhuman expectations and growing shortages of qualified candidates, a career in school administration is for regular mortals. Setting your sights on retaining what really matters, refining what needs tweaking, and relinquishing what has become obsolete create the power and potential to achieve your goals. Clearly, you cannot be all things to all people. Therefore, these pages are intended to help you make informed choices about what you are and are not going to be!

Acknowledgments

Corwin Press gratefully acknowledges the contributions of the following individuals:

Julie Boyd, Principal
Newton-Lee Elementary School
Leesburg, VA

Walter Buster, Professor, Author
Fresno State University
Fresno, CA

Jerry C. Gross, Former Superintendent
Saddleback Valley Unified School District
Mission Viejo, CA

Sharon McClain, Superintendent
Hermosa Beach City School District
Hermosa Beach, CA

Rene Townsend, Executive Director, Author
Public School Services
La Jolla, CA

To my incredible friends and colleagues in Capistrano.
Your hard work, enthusiasm, and endless ideas serve as my inspiration.
Thanks for all that you give to students and to our profession.

About the Author

Suzette Lovely has served as a teacher, assistant principal, principal, and central office administrator in the Capistrano Unified School District in San Juan Capistrano, California, for the past 23 years. Currently she is the Deputy Superintendent, Personnel Services, in an organization that employs 4,500 people.

Lovely has focused her efforts on mentoring principals as well as cultivating aspiring school leaders through her work as an adjunct professor at Chapman University, presenter at state and national conferences, and educational consultant. To provide reality-based experiences for busy site and central office administrators, Lovely has designed the Capo LEAD Academy and the Classified Manager's Institute, which offer separate training modules to help managers build workplace capacity and develop powerful learning teams. Lovely believes that employees at every level of an organization must recognize the unique and important role they play in making their school district a magnet for excellence.

Lovely is the author of the book *Staffing the Principalship: Finding, Coaching and Mentoring School Leaders* (Association for Supervision & Curriculum Development, 2004). Additional work has appeared in a number of state and national professional journals.

The author resides in San Clemente, CA, and can be contacted through the Capistrano Unified School District at 32972 Calle Perfecto, San Juan Capistrano, CA 92675, or via e-mail at slovely@capousd.org or sue.lovely@cox.net.

1 The Information Invasion

If you're thirsty, it's sensible to stand under a faucet, not the Niagara Falls.

—David Lewis, British Psychologist
(as cited in Murray, 1998, p. 3)

Do you ever feel exhausted by the time you roll into the school parking lot, and it is barely 7:30 A.M.? With the sound of the morning alarm clock, most days begin with a cacophony of chatter, news reports, and inconsequential facts and events. At work, the deluge continues as e-mails ding, faxes drone, Palm Pilots beep, and cell phones serenade away even in the restroom. Welcome to the information invasion, where a person is never more than a click away from anything he or she may need or want to know.

When it comes to the transmission of information, modern society has reached its saturation point. It used to be that church, family, and schools were the primary sources of knowledge. People, goods, and news traveled slowly by foot, horseback, or ship. With the advent of the steam engine, followed by motorcars, then aircraft, spacecraft, and finally a little cable known as fiber optics, the speed at which information moves has increased 10 billion times in just over 200 years (Heylighen, 1998). In the 16th century, it took Magellan three years to sail around the globe. Today, a satellite does it in an hour.

GLOBAL COMMUNICATION: FRIEND OR FOE?

Global communication significantly reduces the delay between a scientific discovery and the discovery's acceptance by consumers. At the beginning of the 20th century, for instance, appliances such as vacuum cleaners and refrigerators took 30 to 40 years to reach peak production. More recently, gadgets like CD players, cell phones, and Tivo have swept through the marketplace in a mere decade. Because technology is now so sophisticated, the distribution and production of ideas and information are limitless.

The ramifications of global communication for public schools are devastating if not recognized and managed. When educators are bombarded by academic discoveries, it is impossible for them to see the forest through the trees. According to British psychologist David Lewis, "The fast flow of facts motivates people to a point, but once it pushes past a critical threshold, their brains rebel. A paralysis of analysis [settles in]" (as cited in Murray, 1998, p. 1). Dealing with the chokehold of resources already in existence, while also trying to synthesize a barrage of new information, fuels disorganization, leads to poor decisionmaking, and keeps employees on edge.

One of the biggest problems facing education today is not a dearth of ideas but rather an overabundance of them. It is not uncommon for a school district to have 50 or more changes going on at the central office and even more at individual sites, all within a single year (Kaser, Mundry, Stiles, & Horsley, in press). Lack of quality controls and focus creates unstable goals, deadens creativity, and breeds complacency.

To cope with the increased speed and complexity of technological advancements, educational leaders must become adept consumers. Central office managers can be the first to survey the landscape and find suitable terrain to clear. One worthy exercise to rid a district of debris is to examine the amount of time teachers and administrators spend completing paperwork. Although technology has streamlined many processes, it also heightens requests for more reports and information. An audit will reveal the forces in the organization that generate the most paperwork and for what purpose. Once a list of departmental paperwork demands is compiled, the superintendent should ask, "How do these reports or documents enhance the educational process and improve student learning?" Armed with evidence, the superintendent can facilitate the elimination of frivolous paperwork that is bogging down employees and eating up precious time.

Paperless board agendas are another avenue to save time and money, streamline communication, and maximize the use of existing technology (see sidebar: *Taking the Paperless Concept a Step Further*). An added bonus is that board members model technological prowess for staff and students by showing firsthand how computers are used as a working tool.

Taking the Paperless Concept a Step Further

In 2001, the North Hills School District in Pittsburgh, Pennsylvania, began using electronic agendas for their board meetings (DeMarco, 2002). Faced with four different agenda versions, each numbering hundreds of pages, last-minute additions or changes were nearly impossible and left plenty of room for error. With two board meetings a month, preparing agendas was practically a full-time job for a member of the superintendent's office.

North Hills' Director of Technology and Information Services, Thomas DeMarco, devised a simple plan. The agenda is now put together as a Web page, with supporting documents scanned into Adobe Reader. DeMarco discovered that converting documents to a .pdf file saved time and money and made last-minute changes, such as reordering page numbers or adding charts, a snap. The agenda is loaded onto the district's intranet site as items are completed. This allows for incremental viewing by board members, instead of making them wait until the weekend to read through everything prior to Monday's meeting. Principals and other key staff have access to all but the closed-session items. These most confidential sections require a special access code. Once the entire packet is complete, it is posted to the public section of the district's Internet site.

The cost of going paperless has paid off for North Hills. In the first year, $6,400 was spent on computers, software, and home Internet access for the nine trustees. By Year 2, the cost dropped to $330. In addition, the district has eliminated more than 8,000 pages of monthly copying, and overtime is no longer paid to the driver who delivered agendas twice a month to the trustees' homes. On the night of board meetings, laptops are borrowed from the district's math lab and then returned the next day.

OVERSHOOTING THE MARK

In the Information Age, revolutionary ideas from yesterday are de rigueur today and by tomorrow are already outdated. Although the North Hills School District exemplifies how technology reduces the workload for some, technology is also a source of frustration for others. By the time the latest and greatest equipment is purchased, better, faster, and cheaper machines have flooded the market. This constant reeducation to learn new things can have harmful consequences for school employees. When teachers and administrators are expected to try several unfamiliar products or innovations in quick succession, they become overloaded.

Futurist Alvin Toffler has conducted detailed studies on the psychological effects of grinding overload on humans (Heylighen, 1999). Toffler believes that individuals exposed to rapid and often unpredictable changes develop a sense of helplessness and confusion similar to the effects of shell shock on victims of war. Conversely, when change happens gradually, natural selection keeps all but the most important ideas from reaching people. This makes it much easier to process information. Because progress has no boundaries, many school systems overshoot the mark by introducing too much at once. When administrators and teachers are saturated with stimuli, they eventually crawl into a hole and say, "This too shall pass."

All living organisms have the capacity to fall apart, adapt to changing conditions, and finally transform themselves into something better and stronger. Hardy learning structures certainly do take root in schools. However, without a strong core identity and good filtration system to purge unrelated or irrelevant information, correctly doing the right things occurs sporadically. Reforms overshadowed by other initiatives with more backing or resources simply have no power to ward off resistance. According to the Consortium on Productivity in Schools (1995), attempting to solve problems by adding new regulations, goals, and mandates overwhelms school staff and makes it difficult to achieve any goal. This endangers the support schools need to thrive and undermines the conditions necessary to hold them accountable. The bottom line: Innovation and change are challenging and uncomfortable no matter how well managed they are. But if school systems do not identify specific elements to be left alone, balance and stability shall be overrun by turmoil and despair.

CALIFORNIA'S BILLION-DOLLAR EXPERIMENT

Restructuring efforts in most districts throughout the United States have an abysmal track record. Lack of success is attributed to a number of miscalculations, including (a) little emphasis on research and development to determine why, when, and how something needs to change; (b) the failure to remove structural obstacles; (c) the lack of a critical mass of supporters to lead the change effort; (d) the lack of a clear picture of what the organization might become that looks any better to stakeholders than the one that already exists; (e) the absence of strong leadership to push people beyond the pain of conflict and controversy; or (f) moving on to something new before a change is firmly embedded into the culture (Dufour & Eaker, 1998). When these critical elements are neglected, reforms will not last, since ideas acquired with ease are usually discarded with ease (Fullan, 1993).

A poignant illustration of poor planning and hastily implemented change is California's billion-dollar Class Size Reduction (CSR) initiative, thought to be the largest educational reform in the nation's history. In July 1996, a mere two months before the start of a new school year, the

California legislature voted to reduce class size in Grades K through 3. The initial bill offered school districts $850 per student to create classes of 20 or fewer children. To qualify for funding, schools had to lower first grade first, then second grade, followed by third grade or kindergarten. In addition, districts faced stiff penalties if any single classroom averaged more than 20.4 students over a seven-month period. This unprecedented measure was prompted by poor reading scores; class sizes among the highest in the country; the Tennessee Project Star study, which concluded that smaller classes had a positive effect on student achievement; and an economic boom in state revenue.

Afraid to look a gift horse in the mouth, districts scrambled to hire thousands of new teachers and find space, which was already at a premium. Although funding for the program was the same for every school, the most crowded districts incurred much higher costs and had to reach into their own coffers to purchase facilities and recruit qualified teachers. Sadly, low-income and minority students who stood to benefit the most from smaller classes had the fewest opportunities to participate.

In 2002, the CSR Research Consortium released a study on the effects of smaller classes on primary-school-aged children in California (CSR Research Consortium, 2002). After six years and billions of dollars, researchers concluded that although achievement scores had risen steadily among elementary students across the state, it was difficult to determine what role, if any, CSR played in this improvement. Several factors were noted in impeding the researchers' ability to pinpoint the effects of smaller classes, including:

- Lack of baseline data.
- No comparison scores of larger K–3 classes before the reduction.
- No current state testing program for K–1 students.
- A host of simultaneous reforms introduced at the same time as CSR.

Fallout from the swift implementation of CSR continues to linger. Statewide, the number of teachers increased 46% between 1996 and 1999 (CSR Research Consortium, 2002). This hiring frenzy prompted a jump in the issuance of emergency teaching permits from 1.8% to 12.5%. Making matters worse, noncredentialed teachers are still concentrated in schools with the greatest number of English-second-language and minority learners. In fact, students in high-poverty schools are 3 times as likely to have underqualified teachers, whereas students in schools with the lowest Academic Performance Index are 4.5 times as likely to have them (Center for the Future of Teaching and Learning, 2003). Because of the challenging working conditions, disadvantaged schools have the hardest time attracting experienced and fully licensed teachers.

Another problem with CSR is that operating expenses in most school districts exceed state revenue. As teachers' salaries increase with cost-of-living adjustments and step-and-column advancement, per-pupil allocations have remained relatively constant. This underfunded mandate, which allows virtually no flexibility in averaging class sizes, costs California's Capistrano Unified School District an additional $3.9 million annually. Rising encroachment forced the school board to jettison third-grade CSR in 2003. Although Capistrano parents have rallied together for three consecutive years to raise $1 million and save third-grade CSR, how much more can be expected from the community to supplant the education of children? And what about those neighborhoods that simply do not have the economic means to undertake such a massive fundraising campaign?

Although the program is extremely popular among parents and teachers and has become a sacred cow inside the legislature, are California students really better off now than they were a decade ago? Are the benefits commensurate with the money spent and the sacrifices made to other programs that have been cut to retain CSR? Certainly it is hard to argue that smaller classes are not good for children or that teachers do not have more time to provide individualized support. Yet the evidence is clear that there is no better substitute for a good teacher. An exceptional teacher with 35 students has a far greater impact on learning than a mediocre or ineffective teacher with only 20 students.

LEARNING TO SET LIMITS

As overnight restructuring efforts like California's CSR Initiative sweep through schools across America, is there a way to ward off growing cynicism and create the high-quality learning communities students need and deserve? The solutions lie in setting limits and rationing the time teachers and administrators spend sorting through volumes of information and responding to new ideas. Superintendents and school boards must recognize that information overload and constantly shifting priorities contribute to employee dissatisfaction. If overlooked, an atmosphere of gloom and doom is certain to permeate their organizations.

Most people seek knowledge to perform better in their jobs and gain a competitive edge. On average, professionals spend 38% of their time searching for information (Sage Learning Systems, 2001). Initially, a sense of wonder and excitement is felt as fresh ideas are acquired. However, once the learning threshold peaks, the novelty begins to wear off and fatigue sets in. Compare this to what happens when water is poured into a pitcher that is already full. The added liquid simply splashes over the sides, while the volume of water inside the container stays the same.

Processing an overabundance of information or constantly experimenting with new methods weakens the immune system and leads to what psychologists have dubbed Information Fatigue Syndrome (Murray, 1998). Consider some of the poor first-year teachers you have known (or your own first year in the classroom, for that matter). Armed with a truckload of standards, curriculum guides, how-to books, teaching manuals, and test scores, most rookies are turned loose in September and left to fend for themselves until June. Yet if it were so easy, why do 30% of all new teachers leave the classroom within the first three years and 50% within seven years? Might it be that synthesizing an avalanche of innovations, while attempting to make sense of hundreds of resources already in existence, creates a brain drain? This psychological depletion triggers anxiety, sabotages concentration, interferes with sleep, sparks irritability, and leads to mistakes.

School leaders are even worse off than teachers when it comes to the information invasion. A 1996 Reuters survey discovered that two thirds of all managers suffer from increased tension and one third are plagued by ill health due to overload (Heylighen, 1999). Principals are especially vulnerable as they face pressure to improve their schools yesterday. If they are not overcome by something they are doing, they are consumed with worry about something they believe they ought to be doing.

Are you on the verge of a cognitive calamity? Have iBooks, iPods, and iMovies turned you into a digital diva? To examine overexposure to stimuli, complete the "Are You an Information Junkie?" checklist in Form 1.1. Averting a meltdown may mean a little pruning is in order. Self-assessment is a great starting point to combat information fatigue since a cure cannot be found without first knowing you have a disease.

This checklist reveals how well you are able to ration the time spent sifting through information as well as your ability to set limits on responding to new ideas.

Form 1.1   Are You an Information Junkie? A Personal Checklist

	Usually	Sometimes	Never
1. When new programs or ideas are added to my plate, I find something to eliminate.			
2. I ration the time I spend watching TV, listening to the radio, and cruising the Internet.			

(Continued)

Form 1.1 (Continued)

	Usually	Sometimes	Never
3. I am able to relax when technology makes me wait.			
4. I have learned how to focus on the information I really need by trashing what I do not need.			
5. I respond to e-mail, voicemail, and faxes on my own time once more important tasks have been completed.			
6. I embrace the principle of "just-in-case learning" by spending a great deal of time reading journals, magazines, and doing research.			
7. My office or classroom contains surface clutter in case I need the information for a rainy day.			
8. I spend a significant amount of my day looking for information.			
9. I often feel tense or stressed from information overload.			
10. I have a number of new ideas I would like to implement in my job, but just have not found the time.			

Scoring:

✓ **Questions 1–5:** Give yourself 2 points if you answered *usually*, 1 point if you answered *sometimes*, and 0 if you answered *never*.

✓ **Questions 6–10:** Give yourself 2 points if you answered *never*, 1 point if you answered *sometimes*, and 0 if you answered *usually*.

Interpretation:

16–20 points: Congratulations! You are a critical consumer of information and innovations.

11–15 points: Although you find yourself getting sidetracked once in a while, you have installed filters to sift through what you do and do not need.

6–10 points: You often feel distracted, disorganized, or irritable from overexposure to information. You have not quite figured out when to hit the off button.

0–5 points: You are an information junkie and likely suffer from fatigue and overload! Find the shears and start pruning IMMEDIATELY!

CONCLUSION: TURN OFF THE SPIGOT

Unfortunately, school systems are not designed to cope with the knowledge explosion sweeping across the globe. Thus, many educators are slow to recognize the correlation between this phenomenon and low employee morale, feelings of inadequacy, stress, and burnout. Instead, more recognizable causes for problems are cited, such as shifting demographics, changing family values, undisciplined students, increased accountability, and inadequate funding. Information Fatigue Syndrome is a reminder that too much of something can create disarray inside the schoolhouse.

Sustainable growth in public schools is realized when change and innovation are introduced in measured doses. Since the human mind is not wired to process information in gigabytes, educational leaders have to start abandoning tasks, policies, and programs that no longer support their primary mission of learning. This requires disciplined action in identifying what to give up and what to keep. If the unaltered elements of a system are ignored, even minor adjustments are likely to overwhelm people.

In his best-selling book *Good to Great*, Jim Collins (2001) used the story of the Hedgehog and the Fox to chronicle what distinguishes a good company from a great one. Great companies, according to Collins, are like hedgehogs—simple, dowdy creatures that know "one big thing" and stick to it. Less remarkable companies are more like foxes. These crafty, cunning creatures know many things, but lack consistency. The key to becoming the best at something (i.e., achieving hedgehog status) is to know your core business and then set goals and strategies based on this deep understanding. In other words, identifying what you can and cannot be best at is crucial.

Is your district like the fox, pursuing many ends at the same time, never meshing ideas into a single overarching concept or unifying vision? Or does your organization practice the principles of the hedgehog by reducing all information and dilemmas to simple ideas? In the district of hedgehogs, people know when to turn off the spigot. In the district full of foxes, the spigot is always left on.

2 Teaching Leaders to Let Go

It takes discipline to say "no thank you" to big opportunities.

—Jim Collins (2001, p. 136)

Buried under an avalanche of information, schools are trying to figure out how to churn better instead of more. Unfortunately, most educational institutions lack the discipline to build "fanatical consistency" (Collins, 2001). Such consistency calls for the careful selection of opportunities, rather than the creation of them. Despite some streamlining after the birth of the standards and accountability movement, U.S. schools are still faced with too much to do in too little time.

As leaders whirl inside the vortex of shifting ideologies and burgeoning responsibility, hope starts to wane. Having experienced the leadership spectrum as a teacher, assistant principal, principal, director, and now deputy superintendent, I am keenly aware that putting first things first is a daily challenge. Middle managers are especially vulnerable as pressure oozes from every corner of the organizational matrix, above, below, and in between. Distractions cruise in like heat-seeking missiles, wreaking havoc on already overtaxed institutions. Decisions are clouded by chaos and uncertainty. When Hargreaves and Fullan (1998) examined administrators' responses to social changes and new technology, they found that most school leaders:

- Don't really know how to handle the changes they encounter.
- Have no systematic way of learning about the nature and implications of the social and technological advancements around them.

- Display limited and unimaginative strategies to respond to new information.
- Hold on to perceptions dominated by conventional wisdom, resulting in trying familiar but unsuccessful solutions, or one-of-a-kind initiatives that have little impact on the larger system.
- Possess a weak outlook toward the future.

While schools are under assault, those in charge wonder how to take control of their destiny. No matter how hard they defend against the elements, outside forces continue to dominate daily events and drive decisions. As reactive patterns of thinking slowly waft in, blame and resentment may unknowingly manifest. If such conditions linger for too long, school leaders start to feel helpless. And once they get stuck inside the den of despair, all hope is lost.

BEEF UP COMMUNICATION

Are there ways for a school district to instill a more optimistic outlook among its leadership cadre? Can a sense of control be restored back into the profession? In this era of rising expectations, are there really any tasks administrators can stop doing? Anything is possible if inspiration emanates from the highest places. Through direct and thoughtful communication, rather than coercion, superintendents must listen, tell, and show what is sacrosanct and what is not. Failure to articulate more than vague generalities keeps direct reports guessing as they either (a) try to do everything themselves including the old and the new; (b) make their own decisions about what to discard and what to hold on to, fueling greater confusion; or (c) throw out the baby with the bathwater so that even the good disappears with the bad (Bridges, 1991).

It is easy to lose touch with people when things are in a state of flux. Normal communication channels do not work as well, and the rumor mill kicks into high gear. An honest commitment to empower school leaders with the confidence and skills necessary to let go calls for beefed-up communication. Fabrications, misinformation, or no information diminishes trust and leads to the false assumption that the last assignment or directive is the most important. Administrators prone to constant reaction, instead of action, fail to recognize they have any influence over a situation or its outcome. Immobilized leaders suffer a loss of identity, see themselves as victims, and experience higher levels of stress than their more optimistic counterparts.

As the communication hub, the superintendent and his or her cabinet have to ask more questions, listen carefully, seek opinions, monitor reactions during times of transition, and be available to site personnel. Regular updates about goals and progress help maintain a high level of productivity and keep the spotlight on priorities. If no new information is available, telling people that is meaningful information in and of itself. Even if it becomes necessary to modify objectives along the way, superior results can be achieved if communication is candid and abundant, rather than imprecise and guarded.

Good communication provides encouragement and gives an organization a positive sense of direction. Consider the effects of communication on a group of soldiers engaged in a training exercise to earn a spot in an elite unit (Kouzes & Posner, 1987). The men were divided into four teams and told they had to participate in a 20-kilometer forced march. The first team received precise information about how far they had to go and was kept apprised of progress along the way. The second group was told only, "This is the long march you've been hearing about." In addition, this group received no updates about how far they had traveled or the distance remaining. The third group was initially told they were marching 15 kilometers. But when they reached 14 kilometers, they found out another 6 kilometers had been added to the trek. Finally, the fourth group was first informed that the march was 25 kilometers. But on arrival at the 14-kilometer mark, they learned unexpectedly there was only 6 kilometers to go.

Each team was assessed for performance and stress levels as they completed the mission. Blood tests taken during and after the exercise revealed that soldiers who were told how far they had to march and knew their location en route did much better than their peers. The next successful group was the team who thought they were marching 15 kilometers, and learned at 14 kilometers that they had farther to go. Third best was the unit that was originally given the longer distance of 25 kilometers and later told they had to travel only 20 kilometers. Not surprisingly, the men who fared the worst and showed the highest chemical levels of stress-producing cortisol and prolactin were those who received absolutely no information about the final goal or their progress along the way.

Even achievement-oriented, independently minded school leaders need feedback to remain hopeful and enthusiastic. Regular and specific information makes an administrative team feel they have influence over their journey and strengthens their resolve. On the other hand, communication slippage and ambiguity hurt morale and fuel insecurity among a workforce.

"SELECTIVE ABANDONMENT" AT WORK

In destabilized environments, leaders grow more tentative about their authority and the latitude they have to make decisions. Without clarity, they will try to cover all the bases themselves, flounder in an abyss of uncertainty, or take a "wait-and-see" approach. This lesson played out in our own organization after the Capistrano Unified Board of Trustees introduced *Selective Abandonment* as a key district objective during the 2003–2004 school year (see boxed text). This policy statement was intended to slow down the squeeze on middle managers by empowering them to give up activities that no longer furthered the district's mission.

> ## Capistrano Unified School District (CUSD)—Key District Objective (2003–2004)
>
> Implement *selective abandonment* of activities and programs, when appropriate, due to the growing state and federal legislative requirements and diminishing fiscal resources. The activities and programs to be abandoned will be those judged to have the least impact on CUSD's basic mission—learning.

To nourish a hopeful and resilient administrative team, principals and assistant principals met in "families" grouped by elementary, middle, and high school feeder patterns. Each family was asked to brainstorm a list of three things: (1) the activities or tasks they could control, (2) the activities or tasks they could not control, and (3) the activities or tasks they could stop doing.

As the exercise progressed, only a handful of leaders were able to recognize their capacity to control or give up much. Most intriguing was the fact that veteran administrators felt as uneasy as the newcomers. In each family, similar rationalizations were offered to explain why people could not stop doing things. Myriad fears included disapproval of the board and superintendent, poor performance evaluations, diminished teacher support, and potential parent uprising. (When this same activity was repeated with school office managers, similar results occurred.) These concerns certainly are not unique to Capistrano. Instead, such apprehension simply confirms that as hope erodes in an organization, a new conception of control has to be developed.

Taming the brief, varied, and fragmented conditions inherent in so many executive jobs today, especially inside the principal's office, requires countermeasures in the form of *double-loop learning.* Although *single-loop,* or one-dimensional, learning may offer quick fixes for dealing with a problem, double-loop learning actually produces a change in perceptions, attitudes, and behavior.

According to Argyris and Schön (1974), learning involves the detection and correction of errors. When something goes wrong, the tendency in school districts is to look for other techniques that work better in the present structure. In essence, values, goals, and rules are operationalized rather than questioned. This is single-loop learning. An alternative is to question the structure and variables themselves to try to solve the systemic obstacles that are at the root of a problem. This is described as double-loop learning. Deeper understanding occurs when error is detected and corrected in ways that lead to the modification of a district's underlying norms, policies, and objectives.

An example of single-loop learning is to send a group of principals to a time management workshop to teach them how to combat overload. Newly acquired information will likely have a honeymoon effect as participants perform differently for a brief period. But without continued use or opportunities for reflection, people forget 25% of what they know in 6 hours and 33% in 24 hours (Sage Learning Systems, 2001).

Conversely, a double-loop approach peels away the onion one layer at a time through inquiry and introspection. Prompting school leaders to look inside the mirror rather than out the window is more organic and strengthens the capacity for self-actualization. A well-facilitated process leads people beyond the war stories until they ultimately realize that their own handling of situations is actually perpetuating some of the overload.

Disclosure in the form of double-loop learning does not happen in a vacuum or through the issuance of a new policy or edict. Instead, small and informal meetings with no script or agenda are an ideal venue to let current realities bubble to the surface. Attending to the "nondiscussables" should also be a part of this process (Barth, 2002). Nondiscussables are the sufficiently important subjects whispered about frequently in the parking lot of the central office, in the locker room at the health club, in a darkened corner of Starbucks, or as the carload of administrators crosses the city limits en route to a conference. According to Barth (2002), people are so paranoid that open discussions of these incendiary issues will cause a meltdown, that no one is brave enough to talk about them. Nondiscussables might include the leadership of the superintendent, feelings about how the school board does or does not support management's decisions, or fears among principals that they will be reassigned if their school is deemed underperforming.

Without pushing, probing, or prodding, superintendents may start down the runway believing the plane is ready for takeoff, while the pack of staff is still in the terminal checking in their luggage. If subordinates do not have opportunities to unleash extraneous junk or confront the non-discussables, their "stop-doing lists" are likely to remain blank. The boxed text provides suggestions to lay the foundation for school leaders to start letting a few things go.

Superintendent's Suggestion Box

- Every time a new policy is established, get rid of two old ones.
- Make sure district policies and procedures are written to serve students, parents, and employees.
- Model employee handbooks after Nordstrom's single-rule concept: "Use your good judgment in all situations. There will be no additional rules."
- Do not introduce a new policy or procedure in reaction to one incident—the problem may never surface again.
- No matter the size of your district, no policy or procedure should be more than a few pages long.
- Hold an online auction and invite managers to sell off any negative elements of the culture that are fostering a toxic atmosphere (i.e., idle gossip, biting comments about others, the blame game, incessant complaining), and place bids on the positive cultural dimensions (honest communication, trust, respect, etc.). Share the results of the online auction at a meeting and discuss where the group might go from there.
- Make the disclosure of nondiscussables safe by asking administrators to describe how they sound in other districts. Have people meet in small peer groups and jot down one or two nondiscussables on a card. Shuffle the cards in a bag and redistribute them randomly. Ask each group to offer a few suggestions to tackle their nondiscussable subject.

SOURCE: Adapted from Nelson (1997) and Robbins (2004).

Another important element to unplug perceptions is to debunk the pervasive myth of the all-being "superleader." According to Stanford University Professor of Education Michael Copland (2001), "As certainly as there are a number of .350 hitters in baseball, there are undoubtedly a small number of extremely gifted school leaders who possess all the knowledge, skills, abilities, characteristics, and attitudes portrayed in scholarly conceptions" (p. 532). However, Copland believes that when the bar is set so high, it is unlikely that such rare individuals will gravitate to a career in educational leadership, nor will they exist in the sheer numbers necessary to staff even a small percentage of America's schools.

Last but not least, managers at all levels have to give and receive psychological paychecks to boost morale and sustain motivation. Saying thank you in public has multiple functions beyond simple courtesy, according to Bob Nelson, author of *1001 Ways to Reward Employees* (1994). To an employee, recognition signifies that someone noticed and cared. To the rest of the organization, accolades elevate role models while communicating the standards that constitute great performance. Compensation in the form of praise, promotions, rewards, and celebrations do more for an organization than greenbacks can buy (see Resource A, "Passing Out Psychological Paychecks"). When it comes to the acknowledgment of personnel, superintendents and other leaders should follow these key principles (Nelson, 1994, p. 28):

> **Principle 1:** *Emphasize success rather than failure.* If you are busily searching for the negatives, you overlook the positives.
>
> **Principle 2:** *Deliver recognition and rewards in an open, public way.* If not made public, recognition loses much of its impact.
>
> **Principle 3:** *Acknowledge people in an honest and sincere manner.* If recognition is "too slick" or "overproduced," it loses its value.
>
> **Principle 4:** *Timing is everything.* Reward achievements close to the time results are realized. Time delays diminish the impact of recognition.
>
> **Principle 5:** *Tailor accolades and awards to unique needs of the people involved.* Selecting recognition from a smorgasbord of possibilities enables management to praise accomplishments in an appropriate and meaningful way.
>
> **Principle 6:** *Strive for an unambiguous, well-articulated connection between accomplishments and rewards.* It is important that people understand *why* they are being acknowledged.
>
> **Principle 7:** *Recognize recognition.* In essence, acknowledge people who acknowledge others for doing what is best for the organization.

Treating administrators as a golden treasure instead of just paying lip service to it is invigorating and spawns momentum. As self-confidence and morale skyrocket, a school district moves one step closer to greatness.

MAKE ROOM FOR THE ESSENTIALS

Getting a group of school leaders to change ingrained habits and substitute new ones is a huge undertaking. Despite the best of intentions, individuals tend to revert back to their old ways. Before people can get past the awkwardness of eliminating tasks or duties, they have to understand which programs, services, or activities contribute to an effective school environment and which do not. Since all activities are not equal in importance, a conceptual framework is needed to make room for the essentials. Absent this framework, activities might be abandoned that actually help learning more than hurt it. For instance, scrapping award programs as a way to recapture instructional time could damage school climate and hinder student motivation. Therefore, intelligent neglect—as opposed to blind ignorance—is a prerequisite for the process to work.

Selective abandonment must be engineered as a voyage of discovery, not an all-out race. The goal is threefold: (1) determining which activities, services, or programs to retain; (2) deciding which activities, services, or programs to refine; and (3) identifying which activities, services, or programs to relinquish. Decisions about what to keep represent an investment in the long-term solutions that are bound to have the greatest impact on achievement. Although such benefits may not be realized immediately, practicing selective abandonment with fanatical consistency is certain to mark a turning point in a school district.

Using the Effective Schools Model as a guide, the exercise can be introduced by asking participants to list all the programs, services, and activities currently being implemented or proposed at their site or in the district. Once the list is complete, quality screening indicators are applied to each item. Holding on to a program or activity requires a positive response to each query in the boxed text, "Making Room for Essentials." For an endeavor to be deemed retention-worthy, it has to correlate to one of five benchmark categories, which are also listed. A cardinal characteristic of an avant-garde school or district is their eagerness to avoid the things that do not work and their zeal to protect the things that do!

Making Room for Essentials

Quality Screening Indicators

- Does this program, service, or activity have evidence or data to indicate that it directly contributes to increased academic performance for all students?
- Does this program, service, or activity align with school and district mission and goals?
- Is this program, service, or activity research based?
- Does this program, service, or activity have an evaluation process? If not, can one be developed?
- Do the outcomes and contributions of this program, service, or activity justify the amount of resources (time, money, staff) required?

Benchmark Categories

1. **Student achievement**: Promoting the mission of learning for all students through the ongoing measurement of progress; using assessment results as the springboard for improvement.

2. **Classroom practice:** Delivering instruction through an integrated, interdisciplinary curriculum; devoting time to the skills and content that are valued and assessed.

3. **Organizational practice:** Maintaining a purposeful, safe, and businesslike atmosphere designed for learning; fiercely protecting and allocating instructional time.

4. **Community connections:** Building trusting relationships and good communication with parents and the community to ensure goals and expectations are shared.

5. **Leadership:** The principal and all adults take an active role in the success of students; staff accept responsibility and accountability for promoting and achieving the learning mission.

SOURCE: Adapted from the Intermountain Center for Educational Effectiveness (2001).

One of the best examples of this commitment in our organization is CORE—Capistrano Objectives for Reaching Excellence. In 1996, before the standards movement was launched, and while the California legislature languished in gridlock over a state testing program, Senior Deputy Superintendent Austin Buffum had a vision. His quest: to measure academic growth within the course of a single year so that instruction was really targeted around student needs. In the case of standardized testing, instruction occurs, the test is administered, and results are distributed after students have moved on to the next grade level. This practice has been likened to an autopsy. Buffum surmised if instead teachers were able to determine what students knew in the fall—like a doctor performing a physical exam—teaching could be tailored accordingly. In early spring, teachers would then reassess students and receive new results. This provided a yardstick for growth and left six weeks in the school year to readjust instruction. Working closely with the research team from the Northwest Evaluation Association, CORE was born.

The CORE instructional program establishes benchmarks in reading, language arts, and math for Grades 2 through 8 and uses level testing twice a year to measure student progress in reaching these benchmarks. By assessing youngsters in the fall and spring, teachers and parents have a clear picture of the skills that have been mastered and those that have not. CORE also provides a fair and consistent means across the district to demonstrate student learning over time.

As state content standards were adopted in the late 1990s, CORE was modified to ensure alignment. Around the same time, California approved the State Testing and Reporting program and introduced the Academic Performance Index to gauge districtwide achievement and rank similar schools. Teachers began to question the necessity of fall and spring CORE testing, claiming that students were being assessed ad nauseam. Since the district could not opt out of the state testing program, many teachers requested that CORE assessment be dropped.

After tremendous deliberation, a number of principals and teacher leaders convinced the board to stay the course. Although these feelings were not unanimous, opponents acknowledged that without fall and spring level testing, it was impossible to fully ascertain the impact of a teacher's instruction and to do anything about it while the students were still under his or her tutelage. Since then, CORE has been recognized for its innovation by the California School Board's Association with a Golden Bell Award. But an even bigger testament to the program's success is its replication in districts around the country. Although CORE is not required by legal mandate, it is an excellent way to track academic growth from year to year, which represents a central purpose in Capistrano. It is programs like CORE that should be retained.

For activities that do not receive a positive response to the screening indicators shown in the "Making Room for Essentials" box, a school or district is faced with two options: refine or relinquish. Procedures, policies, or projects in these categories make people feel good, offer convenience, or are showy, but do not directly contribute to increased achievement. For instance, consider the manner in which your organization handles complaints. Parents expect certain things for their children and are not afraid to go right to the top to get them. However, these demands are not always reasonable or in the best interest of students. Some complaints take hours, days, or even weeks to resolve. Quite often, a number of administrators, at both the site and district levels, get involved in dealing with a single community member's discontent. Therefore, a protocol is necessary to maintain a strong focus on customer service without acquiescing on every demand or spending so much time on an issue that learning leadership is completely compromised.

To devise a mechanism for accepting constructive criticism or revisiting decisions while also protecting employees from frivolous complaints, step-by-step complaint procedures—similar to those in Resource B—should be adopted. When disgruntled parents phone the superintendent or a board member without first going through the proper channels, they need to be referred back to the site for resolution. This speaks volumes to the administration by reinforcing an internal, as opposed to external, locus of authority and control. Complaint procedures in many school districts are likely in need of refinement.

In looking for something to relinquish, school leaders might consider all the committees, functions, and community events in which they participate. If volunteering for such activities does not directly benefit students in the school, a designee can be sent or participation should cease altogether. On a larger scale, contemplate afterschool daycare, intramural sports, or home-to-school transportation. Although these are certainly nice services to offer, they do not constitute a core academic function. Nonetheless, they take a tremendous amount of staff time and energy. To relinquish such programs, a district might turn to the YMCA for in-house daycare, partner with a city's parks and recreation department to sponsor intramural sports, or privatize transportation. In addition to transportation, other functions may be outsourced, including the hiring and scheduling of substitute teachers or providing specialized services such as occupational therapy and Braille transcription. Finally, using retired administrators as consultants for monumental projects like the Consolidated Compliance Review or the No Child Left Behind highly qualified teacher credential audit may actually save money in the long run. Although decisions about what to refine or relinquish are driven by board, community, and union expectations, there are always options. What should not be an option is making excuses that continue to leave leaders besieged.

For selective abandonment to have any teeth, the intended outcomes must be explained up front to parents, teachers, and administrators. The ultimate objective is to teach people how to distinguish between what a school needs to do, what is nice to do, and finally what is not necessary at all. Guiding leaders through the Retain-Refine-Relinquish process will enable them to start internalizing the screening indicators and benchmark categories. Then, as new ideas or programs emerge, individuals are equipped with the tools and emotional savvy to take on only those things that support the core essentials.

IT TAKES COURAGE TO SAY NO

We all remember the Just Say No campaign from the Reagan administration. Unfortunately, standing up to pressure is not quite that simple. Behind the reluctance to use this tiny word is the mood of appeasement. To appease means yielding to demands in the belief that once the demands are satisfied, things will settle down. This notion rests on self-preservation and the fear that saying no will hurt credibility or thwart one's popularity. After all, educators are inclined to be gentle, forgiving, and eager to avoid conflict. However, believe it or not, parents and staff do not always expect yes for an answer—especially if *no* is not used just to get rid of someone or if the request can easily be granted. Without adding *no* to their repertoire, school leaders are sure to remain mired in minutia.

In his book *Getting Results for Dummies,* author Mark McCormack (2000) suggested that the art of saying no is easily mastered once people start to believe their priorities are important. To gain a better understanding of when to say no, four basic questions can be pondered (McCormack, 2000, p. 158):

Am I capable and qualified to do what's asked of me?

Do I have time for this task or activity?

Do I want to do this activity?

What are the ramifications of saying no?

After determining that it is acceptable to decline a particular request, the response should be delivered diplomatically. For instance, the next time someone stops you in the hallway with the infamous question, "Have you got a minute?" gather your most assertive skills and kindly say, "No, I really don't. I'm in the middle of something. Unless it's urgent, can I get back to you in an hour [or at the end of the day, or tomorrow]?" If a caring tone is used, few are offended, especially if you get back to them when you say you will. To bypass a commitment, consider the "Five Friendly Ways to Just Say No" in the boxed text. Refusing to be interrupted is a small price to pay for greater effectiveness and satisfaction on the job.

Five Friendly Ways to Just Say No

1. **"I'm sorry, I simply can't right now."** This statement implies that your inability to assist is based upon circumstances beyond your control. Opening with an apology avoids confrontation and softens the turndown.

2. **"I'm going to have to pass on that one."** We all pass on opportunities, good or bad. This phrase says you're deferring the option to another time or simply aren't able to take on the request.

3. **"Thanks for asking, but I'm unable to help you because . . ."** This response tells the rejected person you appreciate their thinking of you, while making them aware you aren't in a position to help.

4. **"So-and-so can help you more than me."** This is a key phrase in practicing distributed leadership. It shows that you have confidence in others to lend support, problem solve, or make decisions.

5. **"Maybe I can do that later."** Use this only as a last resort, otherwise you might be setting yourself up for a similar request in the future.

SOURCE: Reprinted with permission: McCormack, M. (2000). *Getting results for dummies.* IDG Books. p. 160.

When responses are chosen carefully, administrators are consciously abandoning activities that detract from learning leadership. Recognizing that one does not have to say yes to every request is a cathartic experience. If you don't believe it, try saying no a few times and see how terrific you feel!

CONCLUSION: HOPE IS ON THE WAY

Breathing hope back into a weakened environment draws individuals from complacency to action. From the perspective of emotional intelligence, being hopeful means that

> one will not give in to overwhelming anxiety, a defeatist attitude, or depression in the face of difficult challenges or setbacks. People who are hopeful evidence less depression as they maneuver through life in pursuit of their goals, are less anxious in general, and have fewer emotional distresses. (Golemen, 1995, p. 87)

Hopeful leaders are not naïve or complacent (Collins, 2001). They are faced with just as much adversity as others but react differently to challenges than their less optimistic counterparts. By retaining absolute faith that they can and will prevail in the long run, yet at the same time confronting the brutal facts of their current reality, optimistic leaders beat a path to greatness.

Optimism is an attitude that buffers people from apathy and serves as a strong predictor of success. In a study of 500 incoming freshmen at the University of Pennsylvania, students' scores on optimism inventories were a better predictor of their final grades than SAT results or high school grade point average (Golemen, 1995). Although administrators are never going to have easy jobs, districts must search for ways to make a long-term career in educational leadership more attractive and sustainable. Establishing a "critical few" priorities and allowing school leaders to devote the bulk of their time to these priorities will foster a culture of optimism.

To slow down the gradual erosion of energy prevalent among today's school executives, the misnomer of serving as "everything to everyone" has to be laid to rest. Starting with university preparation programs, traversing through professional organizations, and snaking down the corridors of the central office, educators have to accept the fact that the super-leader is a figment of their imagination. Instead of searching the galaxy for this illusory ideal, it is much more pragmatic to teach principals, assistant principals, teacher leaders, superintendents, and central office managers how to cope and garner a sense of control. Doing so relieves excess stress and gives people a fresh perspective.

As leaders look intelligently for tasks to neglect in the midst of endless mandates and relentless pressure, they should ask themselves, "What is the worst possible outcome if I don't do this, and what is the best possible outcome if I do?" Mustering the courage to let go of a little responsibility is therapeutic. With practice, even the greatest skeptics can find a duty or two to relinquish. Without practice, however, the concept of selective abandonment shall remain as elusive as a snowflake in July.

3 Business as *Un*usual

You can want to do the right thing, and you can even want to do it for the right reasons. But if you don't apply the right principles, you can still hit a wall.

—Stephen Covey (1994, p. 136)

There seems to be a growing rift between what school leaders recognize as important and how they actually behave. Consider a recent survey in *Assessing Educational Leaders* (Reeves, 2004), which revealed that administrators have an intellectual understanding of the right things to do, yet they lack the fundamental ability to act on this knowledge. In the survey, for example, 71% strongly agreed it was important to manage time to be an instructional leader, but only 45% said they did so. Three fourths of the respondents acknowledged the critical nature of using data to monitor student achievement and improve teaching; however, only 40% felt they performed this function. Seventy percent stated that educational leaders should "maintain a steady flow of two-way communication to keep the vision alive" (p. 147), but only 27% devoted time to this endeavor. In fact, the single instance where the "knowing-doing gap" did not exist was in operations and discipline—areas that consume the majority of a leader's time and attention. Seventy-five percent were aware they should develop and distribute student handbooks outlining rules, expectations, and consequences, and 73% indeed did. It is likely that if business as usual is reinforced over business as *un*usual, improvements shall be slow and intermittent.

To close this knowing-doing gap, educational leaders have to organize themselves and their work environment in ways to meet increasing demands with greater efficiency. One's own style and degree of organization depend on the level of activity in the workplace, the amount of public contact, the image one hopes to project, and how much effort is devoted to self-improvement. Many wonder what defines personal organization and question whether it is an innate quality or learned skill. If someone's office is tidy and neat, but they are always late for appointments, is he or she an organized person or not? If a subordinate responds to e-mails with lightning speed but never turns a report in on time, is this individual responsible or flaky?

To find answers, organization should be viewed as a continuum. On one end lies the utterly disheveled individual—the person with candy wrappers littering his or her desk, piles of paper everywhere, and hundreds of unanswered e-mails illuminating his or her in-box. This coworker could not meet a deadline if his or her life depended on it and returns phone calls at a speed akin to the Pony Express.

On the other side of the coin rests the Type A fanatic. This individual sets lunch dates a year in advance, has every file in his or her office color coded, and is able to find a document before you even ask for it. When a project is due, it is never less than a week early, and you can bet he or she is the first to arrive at a meeting. The Type A organizer wears his or her Blackberry like an accessory and keeps a daily schedule that resembles a military boot camp.

Nine out of ten people fall somewhere in between these two extremes (McCormack, 2000). So the first order of "business as *unusual*" is to decide where you are on the continuum and where you want to be. A variety of techniques and interventions can then be applied to progress along the matrix. The idea is to identify reasonable outcomes for yourself and be cognizant of your limitations. Without such knowledge, it is difficult to examine priorities and identify attainable goals for improvement.

GETTING INTO GEAR

What qualities define an organized school leader? Do administrators in high-achieving schools have similar or opposing work patterns than their less effective peers? Indeed, there are significant differences in the way successful leaders go about their day. Principals in high-performing schools, for instance, pay far more attention to learning-based activities. In fact, the interruption rate for the most efficient principals is only 2.5%, whereas their average counterparts are consumed by interruptions 5.2% of the time (Pepperl & Lezotte, 2004). Additional variances are depicted in the four graphs in Figure 3.1, "How Effective Principals Measure Up to Peers."

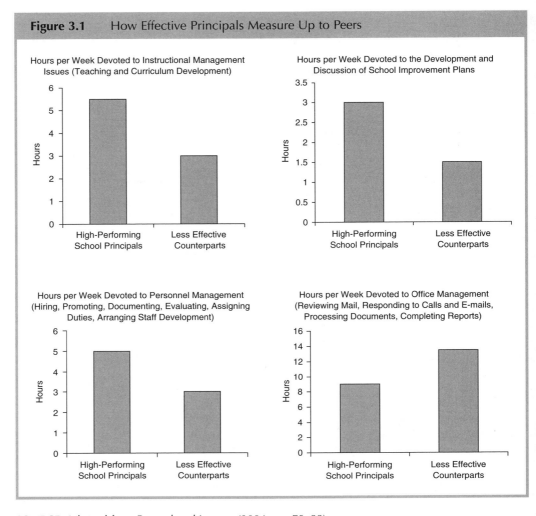

Figure 3.1 How Effective Principals Measure Up to Peers

SOURCE: Adapted from Pepperl and Lezotte (2004, pp. 79–80).

Studies conclude that effective principals are not consumed by operational maintenance requirements. Rather, they plan their day so that most of it centers on instructional priorities. What is particularly noteworthy is that these more successful school leaders are not better equipped than others or surrounded by an entourage of staff. Instead, they are realistic about what can and cannot be done in a 24-hour period, are time and space sensitive, and show discipline in sticking to their organizational agenda.

The welcome news is that personal organization is a craft that can be perfected through practice and commitment. Like any diet, exercise regime, or life-altering program, better results cannot be expected until good habits drive away the bad. To conduct an assessment of your genetic coding and traits, complete the "Testing Your Organizational DNA" questionnaire in Resource C. Once baseline data are compiled, leaders can set about making realistic changes in prioritizing, scheduling, handling interruptions, managing information, and increasing efficiency. There is no better moment than the present to stop spinning your wheels and get into gear.

BUILDING ORGANIZATIONAL FITNESS

Anyone having the opportunity to visit the ancient pyramids in Egypt has marveled at their magnificence and wondered how stones weighing nearly three tons were moved and hoisted to construct such gargantuan structures. Amazingly, the early builders understood that to erect a monument that could be seen for miles, would provide a safe burial place, and would keep intruders out, the mighty triangle was the only design that fit the bill. A pyramid's stability derives from a foundation that is precisely level, arranged in a perfect square, and laid on solid bedrock. With its five sides and strict orientation toward the cardinal directions, it has been said that there is no better architectural symbol for Planet Earth than the Great Pyramid of Giza.

Although no one can predict the fate of public education centuries from now, school leaders have to be chiseled, shaped, and fitted to withstand the test of time. Developing and maintaining organizational fitness over the long haul requires a pyramid of interventions for focused leadership (see Figure 3.2).

As choices are made about what to accomplish, abandon, or abdicate in the course of an hour, day, week, or year, this hierarchy provides a trellis for success. Through a series of applied strategies, a leader's behavior and cognitive processes are stabilized, modified, or retooled. This subsequently reinforces understanding, helps prevent failure, and allows people to reach proficiency with greater ease.

Putting First Things First

✓ Eighty percent of a reward comes from 20% of the effort. The trick is to isolate that valuable 20%. To master priorities, school leaders can apply the 80/20 rule. This means devoting most of their time to those tasks that reap the biggest reward. Some administrators spend hours each week reviewing lesson plans or solving instructional dilemmas. However, findings on achievement-oriented leaders show that more indirect involvement, such as making sure the school runs efficiently, has a far greater impact on learning (Marzano, 2003).

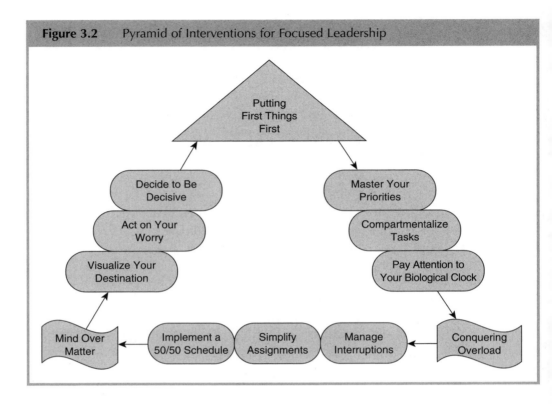

Figure 3.2 Pyramid of Interventions for Focused Leadership

✓ Compartmentalize activities by concentrating on one event without letting another encroach upon your time. If the secretary takes a call from an irate parent 10 minutes before a staff meeting, wait to phone the parent back. This gives the parent time to cool off, enables you to talk to the teacher to find out what might have prompted the call, and keeps your mind clear for the meeting.

✓ Pay attention to your biological clock. If it takes you a while to get going in the morning, then focus your priorities during the latter parts of the day. If your energy wanes in the afternoon, use this time to accomplish things that require less concentration, such as reading e-mail or cleaning out files. Finding your "prime time" allows you to put first things first.

Conquering Overload

✓ Manage interruptions by responding to voicemail and e-mail at select times. Do not become glued to your computer waiting for the next missive to arrive. And give yourself permission to close your door. Although many leaders feel compelled to maintain an open-door policy, this is unproductive. If people know when interruptions are and are not okay, they will learn to respect your time. Hang a clipboard outside your office so that when someone stops by, they have an outlet to communicate their issue. Then be sure to get back to the person before the end of the day.

✓ Simplify assignments so that the endless stream of stimuli is not overwhelming. The soundest advice comes from National Basketball Association star Michael Jordan. When asked how he managed to consistently rack up 32 points a game for more than a decade, Jordan told reporters he broke down his scoring into quarters. Figuring he could get 8 points a quarter one way or another, Jordan concentrated on this smaller feat rather than thinking about an entire 32-point spread (McCormack, 2000). This is an excellent technique for central office administrators to use when scheduling school visitations. Attempting to travel to more than two or three sites a day is fruitless. Instead, stagger visitations so as not to be away from the office more than once in any given week. Otherwise, cancellations are inevitable, making it impossible to get to every campus before the year is over.

✓ According to Doug Reeves (2004), anyone who says that disruptions need to be eliminated during the day probably has not ever worked in a school. Reeves ponders when this might occur: "In the summer? At midnight? In a cemetery? In a school without children?" (p. 7).

A more realistic approach is to actually allow for interruptions by implementing a 50/50 schedule. If only 50% of a leader's day is structured around appointments, meetings, and planned events, he or she has the flexibility to handle unanticipated situations that invariably arise. For instance, it is silly to arrange three formal teacher observations on the same day you are tied up in assemblies for two hours, proceeded by an afternoon Individualized Educational Program meeting. Leaving plenty of white space on your calendar prevents overscheduling.

Mind Over Matter

✓ Form a mental picture of your destination, then arrive there by identifying goals that are few in number, specific, measurable, attainable, and time-bound. Optimal goals are those that cause people to "stretch" but not "break" as they strive to achieve them (Prochaska-Cue, 1995). If your school has an Academic Performance

Index of 750, with an annual average gain of 10 points, setting a target to reach 800 probably is not realistic. But perhaps 765 is doable.

✓ When worry becomes a distraction, do something about it. If you don't, it will creep into other tasks and intrude on your performance. If a situation consumes you with worry, rearrange your schedule so that you can act on it and then move on.

✓ Believe it or not, the ready-fire-aim phenomenon has merit. Sometimes it is necessary to take action, see what happens, make adjustments, and then reexecute a plan. Intuition should be used for smaller decisions and analysis for larger ones. When leaders dare to be more decisive, they boost their confidence and prevent the formation of codependent relationships.

Becoming organizationally fit requires truthful self-evaluation and a commitment to change. By abandoning or altering routines, administrators are able to tackle familiar activities in new ways, making it possible to feel more productive. Thus, the best way to meet the escalating demands for school improvement with less fiscal and human support is to (a) reexamine your priorities to make the most of what you have; (b) conquer overload by expunging what you no longer need; (c) exercise Zen-like discipline to work smarter, not faster; and (d) practice self-control to achieve more of the things you want out of life.

DEPOSIT TIME IN THE BANK

The unrelenting pace of 21st-century living makes it difficult for most adults to ever feel caught up. In fact, the American workforce is being pushed to its limit. A recent study by Xerox and Harris Interactive noted that a majority of people in the United States now work more than 60 hours per week, and 33% work on weekends (Winter, 2004). It is no surprise that there is a huge disconnect between the amount of time educators want to spend on important issues and how much time they actually do spend on them. When time management practices among principals were examined, for instance, the biggest speed bumps were interruptions, scheduling contacts, and dealing with paperwork (Robertson, 1999). Sadly, an inordinate amount of time in schools is spent either playing catch-up or playing hurry up.

• Since time is a constant, there is never going to be more of it. However, there are ways to protect this prized commodity. Rule Number 1 is never give 100% when 90% will do. Although some things are worth doing extremely well, a number of things are just worth doing. Unless you are competing for a berth on the U.S. Olympic gymnastics team or trying to land an F-16 on the deck of an aircraft carrier, perfection is pointless. Taking eight hours to draft a school safety plan that can adequately be written in half the time is inefficient. Devoting two full days to the creation of a 30-minute presentation for the Parent/Teacher Association reaps few rewards. Instead, giving 90% to these endeavors (and never less than that) leaves several hours in the bank. This savings parlays into 100% effort on more meaningful activities such as reviewing student work with teachers, conducting classroom walk-throughs (see Resource A for sample checklist), or evaluating employee performance.

- Rule Number 2 is to pay attention to how often you get tangled in the trivial. Acting on mistaken priorities and reacting to others' demands steals away precious moments from more pressing matters. To make time for what is important, leaders must manage emergencies—authentic or imagined—and spend the majority of time doing things only they can do. When the shipment of office supplies arrives, the computer network goes down, the copy machine needs ink, or the bathroom toilet starts to overflow, time-savvy leaders don't stop what they are doing to get involved. Instead, they rely on the experts to fix these problems while they are off doing something more substantive.

- Rule Number 3 is to practice techniques that permit you to cut corners and accomplish goals in small chunks. An excellent strategy is the two-minute drill (McCormack, 2000). In football, the two-minute drill is used when the offense has to drive the ball a long distance down the field with only two minutes left in the game. Through a series of short, quick passes, the quarterback gets the ball to the receiver, who immediately steps out-of-bounds and stops the clock. There is no huddle, no plays are called in from the sidelines, and no idle chitchat is heard on the field. A good team executes the two-minute drill with skill, accuracy, and concentration. And quite often, they walk away with nothing less than a touchdown.

  Educational leaders can suit up as quarterback and practice the two-minute drill by implementing their own plays, negotiating better times for conversations, completing tasks swiftly, forgetting about making the process look pretty, and ensuring that everyone around them knows the drill. Rather than attending an hour-long department meeting, drop in for the first 15 minutes. When someone stops by your office at 2:53 P.M. as you are preparing for a 3:00 meeting, make your time limits known. If seven minutes is not adequate to address their issue, insist that the visitor make an appointment.

- The final rule to capture time is to x-ray your perspective and attitude. Life in general is a cascade of challenges. Staying dry requires a sense of purpose, well-defined values, and receptiveness toward new ways of doing business. Contemplate how you respond to various demands. Do you work on the squeaky wheel principle, so that whatever makes the most noise gets done? Do you wait until a deadline is near before starting on a project? Do you look for ways to simplify or condense stuff in your life? Do you spend your day responding to others? Do you respect your own time as well as the time of coworkers? Aligning your behavior with your desires is the only way to make every minute count.

Stress and overload manifest not only from having too much to do but also from not completing what is started. It may be impossible to do things faster until you learn to slow down. When a point of diminishing returns is reached, retreat from work to reestablish balance. "It's all about the dynamic of detachment," said David Allen, one of the leading thinkers on personal productivity (as cited in Hammonds, 2000, p. 206). "Sometimes you have to back off and be quiet." Enjoy a respite by walking around the building, watering plants, coloring a picture in a kindergarten classroom, shooting baskets with the seventh-grade physical education class, watching the cheerleaders practice a new routine, or sharing a joke with the custodian. "Desktop yoga" is another option (Queen, 2004). Designed specifically for teachers and administrators, desktop yoga can be done in the privacy of an office or classroom without the need for any special equipment. It involves controlled breathing, integrated postures, and various movements to stimulate relaxation. Participating in self-renewal activities throughout the day is a prudent investment that pays big dividends in the end.

The 10 tips for preserving a school leader's time in Form 3.1. are worth their weight in gold. These tips will assist in setting boundaries and protecting this unrecoverable asset. Effective school leaders are aware that they may be able to do anything, but they cannot do everything. Quite simply, results-oriented people recognize that the problem is not a time shortage issue, but rather a time usage one.

THE BATTLE OF BLIND ACCUMULATION

As knowledge workers, educational leaders face a daily barrage of memos, faxes, advertisements, journals, spam, and e-mail—all reaching their in-baskets at Mach-10 speed (Lovely, 2004). More than 10,000 scientific

Form 3.1   Ten Tips for Preserving a School Leader's Time

1. **Cut out one activity a day.**
   - ✓ Consider what activity you can give up, and then stop doing it.

2. **Never wrestle with a pig. You get dirty and the pig enjoys it.**
   - ✓ Don't engage in a debate with someone simply for the sake of it.

3. **Ask for bulletins and accept only briefs.**
   - ✓ Request a one-paragraph or simple bulleted list to get needed information. Poring over a 40-page document to construct a single memo is unproductive.

4. **Don't double-check what doesn't need double-checking.**
   - ✓ If you ask your secretary to type a letter or a teacher to finish a project, double checking steals away valuable time.

5. **Respect other people's time.**
   - ✓ Avoid interrupting others unless absolutely necessary. Doing this sends an unspoken message that you prefer not to intrude on their time and you appreciate the same consideration.

6. **Choose the right media for your messages.**
   - ✓ Don't send an e-mail when a phone call will do. Don't make a call when a personal visit is necessary. When information needs to be synthesized or reviewed in more detail, send a memo. Tailor communication to save time and avoid unanswered questions.

7. **Safeguard yourself against time bandits.**
   - ✓ To insulate yourself from people who are time thieves, start meetings without them and do not rearrange your schedule to accommodate their tardiness. Handle time bandits like the airlines. Once you call for final boarding, close the door and take off without them.

8. **Keep your boss apprised of your priorities.**
   - ✓ A five-minute conversation or e-mail each day or week with your supervisor can ensure that he or she understands all that you have on your plate. If your priorities are not consistent with the organization's priorities, ask your boss what it is that he or she expects you to be doing instead.

9. **Use a schedule rather than a to-do list.**
   - ✓ A schedule outlines reasonable times to complete tasks and combines a workable to-do list with time management practices. Be sure your schedule is realistic and includes a time frame for completing even the most mundane activities.

10. **Recognize that an emergency is in the eyes of the beholder.**
    - ✓ Keep in mind that not every problem is a crisis. Try not to give in to the shrillest cry. Remember the adage "Poor planning on your part doesn't constitute an emergency on mine."

SOURCE: Adapted from McCormack (2000) and Timm (1987).

journals are published daily. By 2006, the number of e-mail messages passing through the Internet annually is expected to reach 60 billion, up from 31 billion in 2002. A typical manager spends 108 minutes per day reading and sending e-mail (Sage Learning Systems, 2001). As information accumulates, people struggle to do something with it. With a strong sense of responsibility to their jobs, many administrators fear that if they miss an important tidbit or if some new discovery slips by, they will be at a disadvantage. This worry is self-defeating since one's "sense of responsibility" is actually a function of one's "response ability" (Hammonds, 2000). School leaders surrounded by piles of paper, clutter, or electronic junk are destined to be sidetracked and distracted.

Winning the battle of blind accumulation means the chasm between organizational reality and future ideals has to be narrowed. To accomplish this feat, engineering is required in three key areas: (1) Handling paperwork and documents, (2) using e-mail only as directed, and (3) managing space. By effectively using the resources and information at one's disposal, individuals can actually achieve more with less time and effort. After all, no well-intentioned soul deliberately sets out to accumulate a bunch of stuff. It happens gradually and takes over before you know it. Any hope for improving job efficiency requires administrators to exit the paper chase, sail through e-mail, and dump their clutter in the gutter.

Exiting the Paper Chase: When handling paperwork, there are only four options: (1) Act on it, (2) file it away to be dealt with later, (3) pass it on to someone else, or (4) throw it away (McCormack, 2000). Set aside one area at the office or home to process paper. Establish a shelf life for binders, reports, memos, and other documents. Tossing these materials when the shelf life expires prevents paper from accumulating or being strewn about.

As documents arrive, sort them from most to least important and highlight key points for action. Train your secretary to open and examine mail so he or she can appropriately distribute items you do not need to see. Finally, avoid generating more paperwork yourself by using the telephone or e-mail to respond to people. Never write a memo when a phone call, walk down the hallway, or Post-it note is the more practical way to convey a message.

Sailing Through E-mail: E-mail is an enormous distraction if parameters are not established. Without setting time limits for sending or responding to messages, a leader runs the risk of turning into an e-mail pumpkin. Basically, there are only four ways to handle e-mail: (1) File it, (2) forward it, (3) read and act on it, or (4) delete it (McCormack, 2000). To sail through e-mail, click and open items as few times as possible. Use short answers such as "approved" or "disapproved" when appropriate. Delete e-junk straight away, and do not feel compelled to respond to everyone unless a response is truly warranted. Create folders on your desktop to save important e-mails. Printing hard copies of correspondences only adds to the paper chase.

Think about how often you are the recipient of jokes, heartfelt stories, or urban legends flooding the Net. The dilemma is that there is no end to these quips, which clearly interfere with productivity. Deliberate action is necessary to limit your participation (and the participation of employees) in the chain mail brigade. Start by asking friends, family, and colleagues to remove your name from their address book. Then make it clear to subordinates that adding e-litter to an already clogged superhighway is not acceptable during work hours. If you and your staff avoid chatting and gossiping on the Internet, people might afford you the same courtesy.

Last but not least, do not forget cyber etiquette. Messages should be conveyed in a conversational manner, free from sarcasm or harsh tones. What seems innocuous in a sender's head as it is being typed can come across as rude or threatening to the receiver. When all capital letters are used, for example, it sounds like shouting. Long rants are also ineffective. Sentence fragments are okay as long as the point is made, but leave Net speak like "sth" (something), WOT (waste of time), BTW (by the way), and CUl8r (see you later) to the text-crazed teenagers. Spelling errors and textual expressions such as : ((sad face) and : - P (sticking out your tongue) are taboo as well. Always let recipients know the content of an attachment, and be sure to include a topic in the subject line. Finally, under the Public Records Act, e-mails can be subpoenaed and used in formal proceedings. Therefore, anything you say in an e-mail can be used against you at some point in time.

Dumping Clutter in the Gutter: If the insides of your filing cabinets look like a storage unit or the top of your desk resembles one giant tickler system, it is time to rid yourself of clutter. If your work space seems disorganized to you, chances are good it looks twice as bad to everyone else. There is never a second opportunity to make a first impression, so pay attention to the way people react in your space. Then, change it accordingly. After all, who wants to walk into a supervisor's office and get unwelcome vibes?

The best time to deal with clutter is first thing in the morning when you have a fresh perspective. Consolidate and clean out files and storage areas prior to the commencement of a new school year—after you have had time to take a break from it all. Whether at home or work, if an item has not been used in a year, throw it out. Saving miscellaneous items in boxes under your desk or inside a cabinet is a big no-no. Unless something has sentimental value, is of legal significance, or is used with a degree of regularity, it does not need to be kept. If you cannot face tossing that resource binder you were given your first year in management, pass it along to a newcomer or protégé. Keep filing systems simple, with the most commonly used information at your fingertips. And of course, the best tip of all—be sure trashcans are conveniently located!

STOP THE MADNESS

In the allegory *Death by Meeting*, an observer of the company's weekly executive meetings marveled:

> [It's one thing] that these undeniably competent executives can sit through two hours of mind numbing conversation, touching occasionally on interesting topics and then letting them drift away. But to do this without the slightest manner of frustration is another matter entirely. (Lencioni, 2004, p. 37)

Sadly, the public sector is no different than private enterprise when it comes to meetings. With administrative calendars chalked full of them, the obvious result is diminished response times, more things to do, and constant interference with the most crucial elements necessary to educate children.

The madness of meetings can be more torturous than detention. If this is not the case, why do so many people seem to prefer a root canal over a monthly staff meeting? Take a moment to ponder the meetings you regularly endure, be it those you actually schedule or the ones you are forced to attend. Do these meetings resemble wandering affairs that offer a buffet of topics? Do people spend hours talking about inconsequential issues ranging from Big Toy rules, to Homecoming themes, to whose turn it is to clean out the lounge refrigerator? Are the majority of participants held hostage by a small posse of complainers, balloons (pseudo-experts who think they know everything and fill up the room with a lot of hot air), and Sherman tanks? If $1,000 meetings are being used to solve $10 problems, a change-up is definitely in order. Without the stewardship of a disciplined leader, unproductive and uninspiring meetings shall continue to top the list of employees' complaints no matter where they work.

Most staff meetings are ineffective not because they are lengthy or cover a potpourri of subjects, but because they are dull as dirt. If you don't believe it, consider how long adults will sit through a foreign film if the story piques their interest. The touching portrayal of a father and son's struggle to stay together during the Holocaust in *Life Is Beautiful* is a compelling example. After a few minutes, the subtitles are all but forgotten. Although watching a movie is a passive affair and not necessarily relevant to one's life, audiences remain engrossed in the saga because there is conflict, drama, and a problem to be solved. Without a little unfiltered dialogue and pizzazz in meetings, someone is bound to leave disappointed.

If your meetings are as exciting as watching paint dry, it is time to stop the madness. The five structures in Table 3.1, "Meetings that Matter," offer a full-service menu to alter the traditional design of meetings. As sessions are planned, visualize what it is you want to accomplish and then adapt each format to participant dynamics and needs. Remember that bad meetings generate apathy and human suffering that profoundly influence the culture of an organization. Improving the quality of meetings not only enhances staff performance, it also has a positive impact on the esprit de corps. Inspirational leaders know how to take advantage of a captive audience instead of holding an audience captive.

CONCLUSION: DON'T CATCH THE BALL EVERY TIME IT IS THROWN

For those who think that working long hours guarantees job security or spending Saturdays at the office is the price of success, think again. Working harder or trying to do more is an impossible battle to win. With human potential at an all-time high and an overabundance of resources to do practically anything better, "infinite opportunities" are available in every industry today (Hammonds, 2000). Thus, the need for personal organization simply cannot be overstated to spark discipline and resiliency among school leaders—no matter what position is held.

To get to a better place organizationally, the knowing-doing gap must be winnowed away. Although school leaders are intellectually aware of the right things to do, they lack consistency in doing them. Immersing oneself in effective "doing" calls for business as *un*usual. Start by lightening up and making peace with imperfection. Abandon the notion that feeling relaxed at work or leaving the office by 4:30 is a guilty pleasure. Try to concentrate on one thing at a time, ignore distractions—which does not mean being completely oblivious—and do not be afraid to welcome boredom into your work life a few minutes each day. All this enables a leader to come back stronger, sharper, and more creative.

To stop spinning your wheels and get into gear, forgo catching the ball every time it's thrown. Contrary to popular belief, being regarded as the official problem solver or the omnipotent leader is not a compliment.

Involvement in every decision, personal problem, or crisis creates a permission-based work environment. Heading over to the cafeteria to see why the oven is not working is catching the ball. Unless you are an electrician, you are not going to be able to fix it. Answering your own telephone in the midst of four other projects is catching the ball. That's why you have an assistant. Telling yourself that your boss expects this of you is foolish. There isn't a superintendent or school board in the land who doesn't want to see employees function more efficiently, feel less stressed, or cut corners to get a bigger bang for their buck. Business as *un*usual means minding your own business once in a while.

Table 3.1   Meetings That Matter: A Full-Service Menu

Meeting Type	Participants and Frequency	Design and Purpose	What Makes It Work?	Other Things to Consider
Start Your Engines	Administrative assistants; managers; other designated staff; 5–8 minutes daily.	Conduct briefing of daily activities, schedules, or client contacts; review routine items.	✓ Have a standing agenda (don't allow people to sit down). ✓ Keep it operational in nature. ✓ Don't cancel even if some can't attend.	It is easy for busy team members to want to abandon this check-in before giving it a chance. Stick with it and don't exceed 8 minutes.
Oil Change[a]	Leadership team; department heads; 30 minutes weekly.	Define and solve a problem.	✓ Distribute agenda in advance. ✓ Identify most urgent concern or problem obscuring results. ✓ Brainstorm possible solutions. ✓ Use rank-order voting to pare down solutions. ✓ Create an action plan.	Limit to one key challenge so immediate obstacles interfering with progress can be removed. Designate people and time periods for follow-up tasks.
Tune Up	Whole staff; 45–60 minutes monthly.	Enhance adult learning and build collaborative team structures.	✓ Present research or data. ✓ Demonstrate practical use of an idea, program, or resource. ✓ Give peers a chance to apply new concepts together. ✓ Provide follow-up sessions to evaluate effectiveness. ✓ Share results with employees.	Supervisors must observe fresh skills being used. Tangible evidence should be collected that shows improvement to the bottom line. Book shares and journal readings are a great tool.
Brake Job	Small focus group of mixed expertise; 60–90 minutes as needed.	Gather input before moving forward with an idea or proposal.	✓ Have adequate time for people to be candid and honest about their thoughts and reservations. ✓ Heed the suggestions of the group.	Don't be afraid of conflict or disagreement. Without unfiltered debate, focus groups cannot be effective. Limit size to 4–7 people.
Refueling Station	All employees; 1–2 days annually.	Reflect on yearly progress, celebrate successes, and prioritize future goals.	✓ Plan around staff input and district/school growth targets. ✓ Introduce collaborative activities and joint planning sessions to facilitate discovery. ✓ Don't overburden the schedule with lengthy presentations.	Avoid holding event at exotic location that requires extensive travel or overplanned social activities. Be cautious about inviting outsiders. It changes the dynamics.

SOURCE: Adapted from Lencioni (2004).

a See sample agenda in Resource A.

4 The Power of One, the Impact of Many

If thy strength will serve, go forward in the ranks; if not, stand still.

—Confucius

The improvement movement has transformed educational leaders into jacks-of-all trades. The literature is overflowing with qualities today's busy administrators need to be effective. Principals, for example, are implored to serve as stewards, designers, and teachers (Fullan, 1993). While guiding the vision, shaping core values, and fostering a community of learners, they cannot forget to share decisionmaking, link with the outside world, and maintain strong ties with multiple constituencies. And just below the call of instructional leadership is the reality that principals have to manage day-to-day operations. As they supervise the bus line, chase stray dogs off campus, and investigate a sexual harassment complaint, they wonder when there will be time to analyze the just-released test scores, peruse the new textbook adoption, or prepare for the afternoon's Individualized Educational Program meeting.

Unfortunately, the magnitude of accountability facing public schools is only expected to multiply in the ensuing decade. States will continue to establish and then change standards and performance measures, districts will follow suit to meet the shifting state mandates, and schools will scramble to align site goals with expectations from above (Shaver, 2004). This makes it hard for principals and other managers to abdicate much responsibility. Adding to the dilemma is the fact that shared leadership is one of the most neglected elements of professional development for administrators and teachers. A degree of adult dysfunction and denial is tolerated in schools primarily because educators lack the appropriate strategies for working together (Lambert, 2003). Without conditioning, efforts to design an institution of leaders are likely to be unfocused, inconsistent, or ineffective.

LOADING THE BUS WITH THE RIGHT PEOPLE

Great sports heroes understand the power of teamwork. Take former Boston Celtics legend Bill Russell as an example. Russell measured his success on the basketball court not by his own play, but rather by how he made his teammates play. According to Russell:

> Our performance depended on both individual excellence and how well we worked together. None of us had to strain to understand that we had to complement each other's specialties; it was a simple fact. We all tried to figure out ways to make our combination more effective. (as cited in Senge, 1990, p. 233)

This shared commitment propelled the Celtics to 11 National Basketball Association championships in 13 years. No other team in the history of the league has come close to matching this dynasty.

When "Celticesque" synergy flows through the arteries of a school district, the wisdom of working as a whole supersedes any desire for individual triumph. Teachers understand what is necessary to bring out the best in students, principals recognize what they must do to bring out the best in teachers, and superintendents are dialed in to bringing out the best in principals. Not a moment is wasted placing blame, harboring resentment, or worrying about others getting all the credit for accomplishments. Instead, energy is channeled into making lasting improvements. In championship school districts, everyone is in sync.

To build a team with depth and commitment, educators should follow the path of America's standout companies. Instead of using a "genius with a thousand helpers" model of leadership, executives of the most successful businesses make the leap from good to great by first loading the bus with the right people and then figuring out how and where to drive it (Collins, 2001). With this line of thinking, three simple rules apply:

1. **When in doubt, keep looking.** Recruiting the wrong players is disastrous. An organization is far better off leaving a position vacant or

filling it with a substitute than giving a bus pass to an unsuitable rider.

2. **When a player change is necessary, make it.** Keeping bad employees because it is uncomfortable to confront them or too time-consuming to document poor performance can bring an entire organization to its knees. Before you decide to release someone, however, be sure that it is not simply a matter of their being in the wrong seat on the bus. If a seat change isn't the answer, do not allow the wrong person to ride for free. This is unfair to and counterproductive for the right people.

3. **Put the best players on the biggest opportunities, not the biggest problems.** In this way, the underdeveloped elements of the system can get the attention they need. Managing problems makes an organization okay, whereas building on opportunities makes an organization stellar.

Whether someone has the right stuff to join your team has more to do with attitude and character traits than skills, knowledge, or IQ. Recognizing your own style as a leader, as well as the styles of direct reports, allows you to create teams that bring out optimal abilities. Selecting staff members who complement, not compete with, one another is vital.

To glean information about who is riding your bus and their preferred style of play, distribute the personal inventory and supporting materials in Resource D. Once staff members complete the survey and review the style descriptors, the team activity and reference guide can be used to facilitate a discussion on how to increase group effectiveness. Such conversations form the basis for amassing a nucleus of talent whose collective intelligence far exceeds the intelligence of any single member. Authentic teamwork in schools leads to peak performance and is a catalyst for improvement.

P³ = PERSISTENCE × PASSION × PRACTICE

According to Peter Drucker (1994), the purpose of an organization is to make the strengths of its people productive and their weaknesses irrelevant. Masterful school leaders devote their efforts toward the application of Drucker's formula. First, they work relentlessly to uncover obstacles and assumptions that may be hindering a team's progress. Next, they refuse to accept the "potluck" model of training, whereby players have their own workout in mind and expect teammates to take their plan or leave it (Hargrove, 1999). Finally, they execute "cook together" practices so that different backgrounds, talents, and thinking are peeled away and blended into the same recipe. Like a fabulous chef, a fabulous leader knows when to alter the cuisine. This culinarylike experience sends an aroma of shared values, mutual respect, and measurable outcomes wafting through the gym. Games are won as the team abandons any old ways of thinking that breed mediocrity.

Undoubtedly, pushing teachers past the confines of individualism or dealing with a resistant faculty is a struggle, especially in a large school system. Many administrators wonder if it is even possible to get a stuck institution moving again. In other words, is there a way to generate perfect play in an entrenched environment? The answer is a resounding yes. Progress and improvement are realized when school leaders adhere to the P^3 formula embraced by every great coach: persistence × passion × practice. The alternative—quitting—is habit-forming.

The P^3 process requires learning to be layered. Initially, staff members must be taught how to examine complex issues in an insightful, honest manner. Small grade-level or interdisciplinary teams are an ideal venue in which to facilitate candid conversations. In this more intimate setting, conflicts and obstacles are brought to the surface as the leader poses hard questions such as:

- ✓ What is bothering us about this program, requirement, or situation?
- ✓ Is this the real issue on the table or is there more to the concern?
- ✓ Why do we think this is happening?
- ✓ What evidence validates our assumptions?
- ✓ What can we do about it?

The bottom line: Without in-depth probing and dialogue, weaknesses are camouflaged, mistakes are concealed, and assumptions rule the day. Persistence is the key to unearthing what really exists and matters in a school.

Another layer consists of innovative, yet coordinated, action. Although spontaneity is acceptable, teachers cannot roam the campus as free agents. Instead, they have to work in concert to develop "operational trust" (Senge, 1990, p. 236). Such trust spawns intradependence and strengthens relationships. On the Celtics, Russell was able to read his teammates and look out for their best interests because he trusted them. For a faculty to enroll in this coordinated action, a leader needs to address the things that inspire passion. This is much more effective than trying to coerce employees to do something through argument or pressure (Hargrove, 1999).

For the final layer, a staff must actually practice working together. The more that teamwork is encultured into daily routines, the more natural it becomes. Enlarging the sphere of participation has a ripple effect. Conversely, if team learning is confined to segregated units or pockets of like-minded teachers, the results are short-lived. Practice sessions must be inked into the weekly schedule. When educational leaders apply persistence, passion, and practice to scaffold learning, they align a group's capacity to create the results its members truly desire.

Unfortunately, in many school settings when problems surface, the tendency is to blitz right by and start brainstorming a list of solutions. When this occurs, the systemic barriers actually causing the problems are never fully addressed. To avoid this oversight, administrators have to walk into situations and see what others do not. Relying on intuition helps them notice problems and make inferences about their causes. Inferences are then validated through probing questions and active listening *before* any solutions are proposed. Without tuning in to what is happening throughout their building, leaders will have little influence over bringing a team closer together.

ONE PRINCIPAL, MANY LEADERS

Carolyn Williams, a principal in Dana Point, California, offered a poignant illustration of an educational leader applying the P^3 process to harvest a school full of leaders. In 2001, Williams became the fifth principal assigned to Dana Hills High School (DHHS) in less than a decade. With 30 years of history and many original staff members still riding the DHHS bus, it was important that the principal chart a slow but steady course toward improvement. Her goal: To get teachers to work collaboratively and develop common assessments in each discipline. Using the slogan "It's All About You," Williams invoked passion by telling the staff it was up to them to align the academic experiences for students. Knowing this was a tall order, she further explained her role as counselor, custodian, and concierge to ensure their success.

After attending a summer institute at Adlai Stevenson High School outside Chicago, the principal modeled her game plan after the pillars of a professional learning community. Conversations were framed around three corollary questions: (1) What is it we want students to learn? (2) How will we know if they have learned it? (3) What will we do when they don't learn it? (Dufour & Eaker, 1998). Recognizing that change would not happen overnight, Williams sketched out a four-year game plan. After all, getting 122 strong-willed, loosely connected individuals to the championship takes persistence and lots of practice.

In the first year, the staff focused on what the students should be learning. Using the California content standards, each department created curriculum maps. The principal assigned her six coadministrators different disciplines to lead discussions and insightfully examine issues that were an outgrowth of the mapping process. As a former English teacher, Williams linked up with the English department. She observed group dynamics in meetings, redirected people when necessary, and followed up with reticent teachers who opted out of planning sessions. Realizing that collaboration by invitation did not work, the principal also petitioned the District Restructuring Council to seek approval for six late-start days. These late starts, along with a fall professional growth day already in the collective bargaining agreement, provided structured time throughout the year for teachers to reflect on their practice. As a result, teacher collaboration throughout the school started to become a routine obligation rather than a random choice.

During the second year, respected teacher leaders and fellow administrators accompanied Principal Williams on a two-day sojourn with Dr. Richard Dufour, the leading expert on designing professional learning communities in large high schools. Williams fostered confidence and enthusiasm by capitalizing on the group's vast talents. At the conclusion of the training, the principal asked members of the group, "What can we do to bring your colleagues along?" Aware that the leadership team had to provide purposeful guidance without appearing condescending or superior to peers, the principal steered them away from micromanaging the effort. Instead, she offered strategies the core team could use to facilitate productive conversations and build internal capacity. Her suggestions were tailored to address the varied style and needs of the eight high school departments. She reminded the leadership cadre that an important function was to make sure nonmembers' views were heard and respected. Without Williams's sustained coaching and encouragement, the leadership group would have lacked the momentum to bring others along.

The English department group agreed that a subcommittee would draft assessments for each level (English I, II, and III), and then the collective group would fine-tune the assessments. This smaller work unit began by creating a question bank and scoring rubric to assess writing conventions. However, when subcommittee members complained about not having enough time to finish their drafts, Williams quickly intervened by delegating the typing to a secretary. In a professional learning community, the principal orchestrates the abandonment or redistribution of tasks that pose an impediment to achieving schoolwide goals.

In the third year, teachers were ready to start using the assessments. Williams layered the learning in the English department by meeting one-on-one with the 20-plus faculty members and setting individual performance goals aligned with content standards. In this way, teachers' performance goals and annual evaluations were linked to student data gleaned from curriculum maps and common assessments. Once the assessments were administered at the semester, teacher leaders convened subject area meetings to analyze the information and identify strengths, gaps, and trends. A natural outgrowth of this reflection was what to do about the students who were not learning. Various teachers were assigned follow-up tasks such as putting the assessment data on a spreadsheet, talking to students' academic advisors, and researching interventions being used at other district high schools. Finally, stronger teachers were lobbied by Williams to assist weaker faculty members in making modifications in their instructional practices.

The assistant principals watched Williams in action and replicated the process in the other disciplines. By the end of Year 3, the entire faculty reached consensus to add a schoolwide tutorial period into the master schedule. This was a huge concession and would have been impossible without the unified message projected by the joint efforts of administrators and teachers. Throughout the journey, Williams and her team recognized group accomplishments both publicly and privately. And what does this remarkable coach have in store for Year 4? Why, vertical teaming, of course!

Although Mrs. Williams is the first to admit that being a high school principal can be overwhelming and fraught with challenges, she is able to focus her priorities on student learning by relying on others to collect data, complete projects, and make decisions. A testament to her exceptional leadership came in the spring of 2004 when she was recognized as Orange County's High School Principal of the Year by the Association of California School Administrators. In this climate of true—rather than contrived—collegiality, Williams has shown teachers that alone they can do a few things, but together they have the capacity to do anything.

To become the architect of a learning community that houses one boss, but many leaders, follow the guidelines for activating team talents in Form 4.1. If things do not change immediately, be patient. And remember the words of Henry Ford: "Coming together is a BEGINNING. Staying together is a PROCESS. Working together is a SUCCESS" (as cited in Blaydes, 1998, p. 44).

DELEGATION WITHOUT GUILT

As I listened to staff discuss such questions as: Should we close the parking lot at 2:30 to keep parents out? Who will have recess duty when it rains? Is $25 too much for the coffee fund? I wondered how I was going to make instructional leadership the priority of my day.

Form 4.1 Guidelines for Activating Team Talents

Emphasize common interests and goals
Identify mutual interests to expedite the achievement of site/department goals.

Probe the roots of conflict
Allow conflict to surface as a way to improve communication, build strong working relationships, and minimize differences.

Layer the learning
Introduce new information in bite-size pieces so teachers and staff do not feel overwhelmed.

Develop group identity
Provide a sense of belonging through traditions, ceremonies, and celebrations. This builds pride and breeds cooperation rather than competition.

Promote social interaction
Plan socialization activities outside the workday to allow employees to get to know one another on a personal level. When people like each other, they perform better together.

Foster an appreciation for diversity
Expose racial, religious, gender, or generational differences. This spawns acceptance and helps people overcome negative stereotypes.

Dare to delegate
Share the load by permitting subordinates to get involved in decisions and projects. This raises the bar on the level of commitment toward the organization and develops trust.

Spotlight success
Applaud individuals and teams publicly for their accomplishments. When staff members hear about the achievements of colleagues, they feel connected, valued, and proud.

Use "us" language
Rather than *I, my,* or *them,* use language like *us, we,* and *our.* The power to change things rests with those closest to the problem or issue—not with the central office or state government.

It's not a choice
Confront individuals who do not adhere to the commitments endorsed by the team. Ask, "How is your refusal to work/collaborate with Mr. X, Y, or Z helping Johnny learn?"

> After awhile, I realized there were certain things I had to do myself and other things I could delegate. Empowering others to make the decisions about rainy day schedules, coffee funds and parking lots brought me good will.
>
> —*From a New Principal's Perspective* (Pruitt, 2003, p. 11)

Whether you work in a school or the central office, if others are not entrusted to act, managers' successes are limited to only those tasks they can perform on their own. Trying to do everything yourself is not only unreasonable, it is physically impossible. With America's future resting on the ability of educators to turn out students who will build a better tomorrow, school leaders must expand leadership capacity and learn to delegate without guilt. Otherwise they will labor to finish assignments they are good at with any degree of consistency.

Because teachers are the largest, most influential group in a school, they should assume the majority of responsibility (Lambert, 2003). This does not mean that every teacher is expected to contribute in exactly the same way. Some can take on more modest roles than others. For example, a first-year math teacher probably is not the right choice to chair the committee to develop the eighth-grade algebra road map. Yet he or she may be ideal for coordinating Family Math Night. A seasoned teacher with a flair for scheduling can be called on to help the assistant principal build common preparation periods into the master schedule. An exceptional organizer might be enlisted to facilitate student study team meetings. Finally, a skilled mentor can be invited to serve as a peer coach and assist a veteran who is struggling with classroom management. In other words, teacher leaders have to be cultivated in accordance with their talents and interests. Checkpoints must be incorporated along the way to guarantee their success. Finding tasks that suit each teacher best allows every member of a faculty to experience a sense of accomplishment.

When employees refuse to accept assignments because "they are management's job" or constantly seek permission to do things, it may be because the supervisor is behaving in an authoritarian, albeit benevolent, manner. To develop a dynamic learning community, leaders have to give up power and permit staff to make decisions. Although most administrators are aware that a "tell and command" approach suppresses shared leadership, some still fear that relying too heavily on subordinates will cause a loss of control, be viewed as a sign of weakness, or reflect poorly on them if mistakes are made. Of course, such misconceptions trick leaders into thinking they hold a license on knowledge and expertise that others don't. Dismissing the capabilities of staff in such fashion is not only demeaning, it is counterproductive as well.

Delegation is an ethical responsibility leaders owe to themselves, their employees, and their organization. For supervisors, delegating provides more time for planning and organizing, engenders trust, and facilitates open communication. For employees, it builds self-esteem, fosters creativity, and offers training in skillful leadership. For the organization itself, delegation increases productivity, stimulates learning, and promotes a positive climate. Delegating is not about giving people more to do or about assigning all the unpleasant duties to someone else. That's called dumping. Instead, delegating is about prompting others to get involved by capitalizing on a group's broad talents and experiences. When managers dare to delegate, employees grow personally and professionally, and their confidence as leaders soars!

Many people who hold positions of power are reluctant delegators. Concerns range from "Who has time to delegate?" to "Aren't I giving up my authority?" to "If I have to ask for help, won't people think I'm not doing my job well?" Done correctly, however, delegating has a multiplier effect. In fact, Thomas Edison credited his success as an inventor to this phenomenon (Schmoker, 1999). By placing his workers near one another, scientists were able to consult on their projects. Edison's staff not only performed better than their counterparts, they worked more quickly and efficiently as well.

To determine your comfort level in delegating responsibility to others, take the delegation quiz in Form 4.2. Then use the Dare to Delegate checklist in Form 4.3 to hone in on areas for improvement. Remember, when leadership is shared, common goals are achieved. Knowing how to manage delegated tasks and getting commitments from others to do what they say is the ultimate way for a leader to shine.

Since there is plenty of work to be done in schools, delegation affords a larger number of people the chance to assume formal leadership roles, permits several projects to be completed simultaneously, and increases the quality of the end result. When administrators delegate, responsibility is equitably—not equally—distributed among those with a vested interest in the outcome. Delegating combats employee isolation, reduces fatigue, and lessens the chance for burnout. What better way to keep both supervisors and staff from spreading themselves too thin?

Form 4.2   Delegation Quiz

True	False	What makes it hard for *you* to delegate? Take the following quiz, then use the Interpretation to reflect on your skills and confidence in practicing distributed leadership.
T	F	**1.** I'm too busy to delegate. Explaining a task simply takes too much valuable time.
T	F	**2.** I can do most things better and faster myself.
T	F	**3.** The people I delegate to will get all of the credit. Others in the school community may think they are more qualified than me.
T	F	**4.** I am afraid the person will botch the job.

(Continued)

Form 4.2 (Continued)

True	False	What makes it hard for *you* to delegate? Take the following quiz, then use the Interpretation to reflect on your skills and confidence in practicing distributed leadership.
T	F	**5.** I fear my staff might think I am making them do more work.
T	F	**6.** I'm not sure if this is an assignment that can be delegated.
T	F	**7.** My superintendent/boss may disapprove of me delegating a task he or she has given me to do.
T	F	**8.** If someone wants to assist, they will let me know. I shouldn't have to ask for help.
T	F	**9.** If I complete projects myself, I don't have to worry that they won't be finished on time.
T	F	**10.** It just never occurred to me to ask anyone for help.

DELEGATION QUIZ—INTERPRETATION

1. If you answered "true," consider how ridiculous this actually sounds. If you are being inundated by tasks, you simply cannot afford *not* to delegate. Otherwise you will continue to feel overloaded at work.

2. If you answered "true," stop and think about whether it is more important to get the job done exactly as you would do it or to help others learn to do the job. Think about how much patience you have and whether you are willing to share your knowledge with others.

3. If you answered "true," examine your confidence level. Do you secretly underestimate your potential as a leader? Remember, your boss already has faith in your abilities or you would not have gotten the job in the first place.

4. If you answered "true," consider what is the worst thing that could happen. What safeguards can you build into the role to feel better about delegating?

5. If you answered "true," remember that your trust in someone's ability to do a project is the greatest compliment you can give. When people get recognition and support from their supervisor, the results get geometrically better.

6. If you answered "true," consider that common sense goes a long way here. If it does not involve privileged information or setting policies, then it probably can be delegated.

7. If you answered "true," you may be surprised that your superintendent wants you to delegate more. He expects you to use the people who report to you to get the job done—not to do everything yourself.

8. If you answered "true," you are thinking reactively instead of proactively. Your staff usually does not realize how busy you are or what you are in the midst of unless you tell them. Expecting unsolicited assistance may be the onset of "victimhood."

9. If you answered "true," you probably have forgotten how many other things you are working on right now. When you face an overabundance of assignments and duties, it is likely you won't make all the deadlines either.

10. If you answered "true," it's time for you to take a step back and reflect on your position and responsibilities. You are moving so quickly from one activity to another, you haven't even realized you are spinning your wheels.

CONCLUSION: BRING HOME THE YELLOW JERSEY

In high-achieving organizations, the functions of leadership resemble a web with the positional source of power resting in the center. The web symbolizes a nonhierarchical distribution of authority and control. It is spun at each school site or in every division so that if the supervisor falls, he or she is supported. In this environment, administrators are keenly aware that leadership is learned and shared, not a birthright or enthroned. Thus, they work to ensure that every staff member is involved in the drive toward excellence.

A parallel approach to distributed school leadership is found in the world of cycling. The top riders on each team are surrounded by *domestiques* who provide protection in the peloton and pull teammates along when they lag behind. These selfless members of the pack take turns playing a subordinate role. In any given race, they are primarily there to back up their team and its best competitor. Although domestiques spend time in the shadow of the leader, they understand and take pride in this assignment. World-class cyclists rely on domestiques to save their legs for the big climb, chase down the breakaway, or attack off the front. Without these faithful comrades, neither the team nor their leader stands a chance.

Form 4.3   Dare to Delegate Checklist

Complete the checklist below to determine the areas you need to focus on in improving your delegation skills.	Yes	No
1. Do you decide what you can delegate?		
2. Do you break the task into the smallest possible pieces?		
3. Do you form a mental picture of each completed task?		
4. Do you select the tasks you must do yourself?		
5. Do you assess the skills of the people to whom you will delegate tasks?		
6. Do you assess the interests of these people?		
7. Do you assign the tasks based on skills and interests?		
8. Do you assign the authority and limits of discretion so the task can be completed?		
9. Do you identify who will do the task?		
10. Are you specific about what it is you want done?		
11. Do you determine why you want a particular person to perform a task?		
12. Do you decide when the task must be completed?		
13. Do you explain what the completed task will look like?		
14. Do you ask questions to ensure understanding?		
15. Do you inform others who need to know about the assignment?		
16. Are you enthusiastic about delegated activities?		
17. Do you monitor the progress of various assignments at regular intervals?		
18. Do you require feedback?		
19. Do you provide feedback?		
20. Do you reward others for a job well done?		

SOURCE: Adapted from Lemley, Howe, and Beers (1997).

The team leader, on the other hand, is a savvy rider. His or her training focuses on the output of power, rather than speed or distance. In a bike race, cadence is a more accurate gauge of performance than miles per hour. Throughout the season, endurance, strength, and confidence are built to face the mother of all races—the Tour de France. Peddling 2,200 miles in 21 days takes brawn, brains, and humility. Lance Armstrong recognizes the power of one and impact of many. He has won an unprecedented seven Tours because he intuitively knows when to sit back and take advantage of the draft, when to remain insulated in the peloton's cocoon, and when to let someone else have the stage. Armstrong also bestows credit where credit is due. Whether it is his own teammate or an opponent doing most of the work on a given day, Armstrong shares his appreciation with the press as well as fellow athletes. Surrendering the yellow jersey to a competitor is not a problem either because everyone is aware that wearing it only matters in one place—on the Champs Elysees.

Let's face it: School leadership is a test of stamina and mental fortitude. Like the Tour de France, the course is rugged, is meandering, and changes from year to year. Reaching the finish line comes from spinning a web of support, letting teammates take turns riding in the front, and sharing the glory along the way. Without a cohesive unit, bringing home the yellow jersey is nothing more than a pipe dream.

Imagine how monotonous life would be if the same one or two people got to be in charge all the time and make up all the rules. Instead of worrying about how much work there is to do, start permitting others to do some of the work. When leaders allow subordinates to become the experts, they put their team on the road to a championship season.

5 Getting a Grip on Data

We're drowning in information and starving for knowledge.

—Rutherford D. Rogers
(as cited in Blaydes, 1998, p. 35)

Data here; data there; data, data everywhere! According to Marzano (2003), the current era of school reform is characterized by heavy doses of data. In fact, school systems are expected to collect nine times as much information as other major corporations (Anderson, 2004). Daunting requirements for a system whose primary mission is teaching and learning—not data compilation and analysis—make it hard for educators to keep their heads above water.

Without question, the use of data sets the stage for cogent discussions and ultimately leads to meaningful outcomes. This is good for schools and good for children. So what seems to be the problem? With a mother lode of data waiting to be mined, educators are struggling to hit the right vein. If making data-based decisions is a defining characteristic of school improvement, then leaders have to know how to collect, organize, analyze, and use data. Without a firm grip on data selection and examination, the requirements to generate reports and information about students shall take precedence over educating them.

EXCAVATING QUALITY DATA

The expression "Schools are data rich and information poor" describes the phenomenon that although a plethora of facts and figures are available in school systems today, very little is actually used to alter the way things are done (Holcomb, 2004). In fact, public education has been reinventing itself for years without really changing much. Although site administrators are further down the road to data acceptance and use, central office leaders seem to lag behind. It may be that the folks in transportation, food services, maintenance and operations, or personnel "don't do data" as well simply because they are not required to base decisions on it. Although district support staff are awfully good at producing reports and requesting information from schools, this material is not regularly evaluated to inspire their own operations. Exemplary school districts, however, use data to spotlight strengths and unearth weaknesses in every department. Information is then applied to pave a path toward improvement.

To excavate quality data, school leaders—especially those in a central office role—must figure out what information is available and how knowledge will be gleaned from this information. Aside from raising test scores, data might be needed to reduce districtwide utility costs, increase sales of school lunches, or enhance the efficiency of a given department. To prevent data smog from polluting the skies, discipline is paramount. Contaminated data are worse than no data at all since the absence of information means an organization will likely maintain the status quo. Flawed data, on the other hand, prompt changes or decisions based on faulty assumptions. This can have devastating consequences for students as well as employees. The essential questions in Form 5.1, "Mining Good Data," should serve as the litmus test in determining what data are necessary, what data are nice, and what data have got to go.

TAKE THE PLUNGE

There is no need to fret that a degree in statistics is necessary to decipher data. Any conscientious soul who can count, calculate, and think has the ability to take the data plunge. The best advice for any workplace is to start small and capitalize on what is at hand. As skills and confidence develop, exploring the deeper parts of the mine will come naturally. Depending on the readiness level of a department or team, leaders might consider one of the following methods to get the process under way:

The Snapshot Technique. The Snapshot Technique involves identifying a simple piece of data to increase a staff's comfort level in using it. This worked well in my own division after a spike in worker's compensation claims in 2003. An easy piece of data to collect was the breakdown of claims by job classification. In doing so, the insurance office found that special education aides experienced the largest jump in work-related

Form 5.1   Mining Good Data

1. **Do the data deal with the district's most immediate concern?**
   If the answer is yes, then this is information the district needs to know. If the data deal with an issue the district plans to address in the future, then they are nice-to-know data. If the district could care less about the information, the data are useless.

2. **Is the district better equipped to make a decision because of these data?**
   If the answer is no, is it a nice tidbit to file away for later? If not, the data are not worth the paper they are printed on.

3. **Has time been saved or wasted by having this information?**
   If decisive action can be taken as a result of having these data, then it is worth the time and energy to collect and analyze them. If not, don't bother.

4. **Did (or will) the data lead to positive future action?**
   If a data nugget leads the organization to the vein where the mother lode lies in wait, go for it. This information definitely has value and is worth pursuing.

5. **Does the organization need this information to accomplish its goals?**
   Consider how widely the data are going to be used by staff and how they will assist in achieving major district objectives.

SOURCE: Adapted from McCormack (2000).

injuries. Further digging revealed that more paraprofessionals had been hired that year, and many were assigned to work with autistic children. When these youngsters flailed during behavioral outbursts, the aides were hurting their backs trying to lift or reposition students. This snapshot of information prompted the insurance department to lobby the personnel office to put safeguards in place that would reduce the injury rate of these employees. Easy fixes involved revising the job description to include minimum lifting requirements, preemployment physicals, and injury prevention training for existing aides.

The Organic Approach. The Organic Approach concentrates on a combination of sources to meet an objective or solve a dilemma. Let's say the transportation department wants to cut overtime costs by 5%. Managers and shop stewards should jointly decide what information is most relevant to achieve this goal. The process might begin by breaking down monthly overtime expenses via driver and route. Pinpointing where the overtime is coming from generates questions about why it is happening. As anomalies are discovered, additional research is conducted, such as studying contract provisions, identifying routing glitches, or examining cocurricular busing schedules. The organic approach allows an assortment of information to surface from the inside out and lets staff closest to the problem find the right mixture to fix it.

The No Excuses Option. The No Excuses Option focuses on addressing a problem by using reports that are required by law. Whether it is the number of highly qualified teachers employed in your district, state-adopted test scores, or dropout rates, everything is reportable nowadays. Since there is no hiding bad news, the No Excuses Option pushes staff toward accountability without finding fault. As upsetting as it is to read in the newspaper that your school is failing, sometimes it takes negative publicity to nudge employees along. Consider the hot topic of school safety. Under No Child Left Behind (NCLB), students in "persistently dangerous" schools can transfer to another site in the district. Since each state gets to define what characterizes a persistently dangerous school, a safe campus in Illinois may be deemed unsafe in Colorado. Although such distorted data seem unfair, they nonetheless cause the public to judge whether a school is good or bad. It is up to the faculty, then, to find ways to make their facility safer. Whether it means reducing the number of student fights—which are often reported as assaults—or cracking down on vandalism, there can be no excuses for maintaining the status quo.

The Event-Based Tableau. In this scenario, information is generated around specific incidents and events rather than test scores or demographics. The Event-Based Tableau calls on staff to look at a particular situation, such as student discipline or employee attendance, to get a long-overdue wake-up call. For instance, while the overburdened assistant principal self-destructs in his or her office dealing with endless discipline referrals, teachers are oblivious to the fact that their lack of classroom structure is exasperating the problem. Or unbeknownst to a teacher who cherishes his or her monthly mental health days, studies confirm that learning suffers under the tutelage of substitutes. Confronting a faculty with event-based data forces them to see patterns in student behavior as well as their own behavior. This then becomes the impetus to modify or better manage certain practices and events.

The Customer Service Model. The Customer Service Model is one of the more difficult data maneuvers to master. Going right to the source to garner stakeholder opinions or desires and then altering the way you do business as a result takes institutional maturity. Yet taking customers for granted, relying on past successes, or assuming everyone wants the same thing has caused the demise of the best of organizations. Therefore, finding out how customers feel about a particular issue may prevent heartache down the road.

It is probably obvious that changing a district calendar, redrawing attendance boundaries, or closing down a campus will send a school community into a tailspin. But messing with the school parking lot, picking a new mascot, or moving the principal can also create a frenzy. Before making landmark changes, consultation with customers is critical. Measuring customer satisfaction through surveys, listening tours, public hearings, or advisory groups provides great sources of feedback. Recognizing what customers value and expect is an integral part of sound decisionmaking.

Results-oriented leaders not only decide which data are relevant, they develop strategies for exposing staff to this information. They know the bottom line and work backwards to control how much detail is undertaken at once. Each data snippet is carefully judged to determine whether it will move people closer to or further away from the organization's goals. If information is not going to hasten student achievement or spawn improvement, it is discarded. However, when learning is at a standstill, money is going down the drain, or time is being frittered away, effective managers do not hesitate to put their foot down. By forcing subordinates to choose their pain—either the pain of growth or the pain of decay— dataphobics are apt to get the message that avoidance is not an option.

TURNING DATA INTO KNOWLEDGE

Once a team finds itself moving toward the danger, it is the leader's job to ensure that group does not become lost in the translation. If a school or department maintains a stockpile of colorful charts, tables, or graphs without any clue as to what to do with them, they are just as bad off as if they had no documents at all. When it takes years for an initiative to get under way because people are stuck in the quicksand of planning, what good is the initiative? Turning data into knowledge requires early momentum, ongoing attention, and a culture that views disclosure as a way to shape a better future.

A two-year research study by the University of Wisconsin (Mason, 2002) noted six key obstacles educational systems face in transforming data from dull stones into gems of radiance and beauty. Awareness of these barriers makes the data trek less contentious as school leaders attempt to steer people in the right direction.

1. Cultivating the desire to transform data into knowledge. Momentum, time, and resources are necessary to foster an environment that incorporates data into the life of an organization. No matter who lays the foundation, committed leadership is essential to support a workplace that looks at evidence to uncover the root causes of problems. Information must be open, honest, and accessible. Meaningful dialogue and professional development play a significant role in transforming data into knowledge that ultimately enhances performance.

2. Focusing on process for planned data use. If information is gathered in a haphazard manner or has no specific purpose, employees will view its collection as a lesson in futility. Avoiding this pitfall calls for data compilation to be linked directly to the improvement process. If a leader or work team first outlines how certain data will be used, staff members are more likely to draw conclusions that explain why something is or is not happening. As a result, priorities and goals can be properly refined.

3. Committing to the acquisition and creation of data. Inputting and retrieving data into a usable format is a huge challenge, especially if central office databases and site systems do not talk to one another. Quite often, schools have to call the district's testing coordinator or technology department to get reports. The technology infrastructure should facilitate the easy collection, maintenance, and storage of important information. Without a means for employees to readily access data, it will remain too cumbersome for most to bother.

4. Managing and organizing data. Questions loom about who will enter and maintain certain data fields, how confidential student and employee files will be protected, which computer systems will warehouse information, and whose responsibility it is to download data from the central office onto the appropriate software. Before information is ever reviewed or reported, someone has to enter it, secure it, update it, download it, and format it. Decisions about "who" and "how" must be handled up front, otherwise the flow of data is constantly stalled by these dilemmas.

5. Developing analytical capacity. Considerable training is necessary for a staff to be able to select the appropriate indicators that expose strengths, weaknesses, and trends. Practice is also required to properly interpret and apply these results. Some work sites are tackling the problem by identifying "data mentors" to serve as building-level experts (Nicols & Singer, 2000). By equipping a small team with precise diagnostic tools, shared expertise is created and then used to train others. As capacity spreads among a staff, varying levels of knowledge develop. Ongoing connections to site goals strengthen people's ability to relate to data. This sends a cogent message that using data is everyone's responsibility.

6. Strategically applying information and results. The analytical process has to be transparent and unbiased so that the truth is revealed—no matter how disappointing it might be. Conclusions can be drawn only from accurate, valid, and reliable measures. For employees to find value in the information and accept responsibility for making improvements, the evidence cannot be used against them. Inflammatory or inaccurate data discourage people from ferreting out the facts. Furthermore, if individuals are sanctioned or punished because of the information, they will put their own spin on the results or, even worse, sabotage the process. Outcomes should highlight progress, lead to the exploration of problems, and target specific areas for growth.

To demystify data, staff need to be shown how certain information is actually going to make their jobs easier. Relying on one or two wizards to compile and interpret reports to the exclusion of others gives the impression that only smart people are capable of working with data. To bring the process into the mainstream, each data dig should be (a) congruent with the organization's vision and goals, (b) accurate and complete, (c) based on multiple measures, and (d) inclusive of short-term results. Like the soldiers in the training exercise described in Chapter 2, if a group knows where it is going and how participants are faring along the way, they are more likely to arrive at their destination in a healthy state of mind.

The Data Barriers Inventory in Form 5.2 pinpoints obstacles that may exist in your current work setting and reveals the degree to which these obstacles are interfering with progress. As leaders begin to comprehend why employees are holding back, each barrier can be confronted and ultimately removed. Making data collection and analysis less threatening allows a team to turn information into valuable knowledge that will truly make a difference.

Form 5.2   Data Barriers Inventory

Directions: Read each of the data barriers listed, and circle the number you believe most accurately reflects what is currently happening in your work setting. These barriers represent common technology, opportunity, and knowledge challenges school systems face in attempting to use data. Be candid in your responses.

1 **Strongly descriptive** of my work site
2 **Descriptive** of my work site
3 **Slightly descriptive** of my work site
4 **Not at all descriptive** of my work site

1. The work culture does not focus on data.	1 2 3 4
2. Gathering data is perceived as a waste of time.	1 2 3 4
3. Few, if any, people in my school/department are adequately trained to gather and analyze data or maintain databases.	1 2 3 4

4. Employees think it is not their job to analyze data.	1 2 3 4
5. Supervisors do not direct subordinates to collect or review data.	1 2 3 4
6. Technology is outdated or inadequate.	1 2 3 4
7. Appropriate, user-friendly software is not available.	1 2 3 4
8. Staff members have had only negative experiences with data.	1 2 3 4
9. Staff members feel threatened by data.	1 2 3 4
10. There are not enough examples of how our department or site might collect, maintain, or benefit from the use of data.	1 2 3 4

Interpretation:

Total the responses to the 10 statements to determine how important data compilation and analysis are perceived as being in your workplace. Then review the following solutions to challenge the existing culture, improve productivity, and enhance the quality of learning for students *and* adults.

30–40 **Strong data culture:** Decisions are continually centered on data and results.

20–29 **Moderate data culture:** Capacity exists to turn data into knowledge. People are beginning to recognize the value of data.

10–19 **Progressing data culture:** Pockets of employees are learning how to collect and apply data, but data are used sporadically.

1–9 **Weak data culture:** Data are not factored into the decisionmaking process at all.

SOLUTIONS FOR OVERCOMING OBSTACLES

- Scrutinize existing data-gathering processes and make necessary adjustments.
- Share examples of how people can save time and resources by reviewing certain pieces of data.
- Identify specific and measurable outcomes for data use so that employees can gauge their success.
- Decide up front what you want to do with the information.
- Develop a data collection plan and determine which elements will be used as performance indicators.
- Build time into the workday for employees to peruse and talk about data.
- Identify one or two data mentors who can train others in the process.
- Organize data by topic (content, correlates, or essential questions).

- Create a system for the physical organization and storage of data—file folders, data boxes, spreadsheets, individual notebooks, and school portfolios.
- Establish specific questions to answer as data are triangulated and disaggregated.
- Design site improvement plans based on the information uncovered.
- Regularly communicate progress to staff and others.
- Celebrate gains—both large and small.

SOW THE SEEDS OF SUCCESS

To establish a reasonable accountability system, the ability to harvest good data should be doable for the average employee. If expectations are beyond human reach or wins occur sporadically, people will lose interest or worse—they'll stop trying. Experts agree that less dramatic improvements that represent incremental growth are just as crucial as huge gains that happen infrequently (Schmoker, 1999). By honing in on smaller victories, data management is not as intimidating. Without sustained enthusiasm, however, employees may be able to get a grip on data but they will not hold on for long.

Sowing the seeds of success means that data cultivation cannot be a feast-or-famine endeavor. Getting a staff focused and excited requires that progress is regularly monitored and adjustments are made based on results. As priorities are set in motion, the following guidelines serve as a catalyst for building employee confidence and allaying any fears of failure:

- **Do not use data simply to rid a school or department of poor performers.** Such action sends terror through an organization and encourages avoidance or the fudging of facts. When this tactic is used, it is commonly the best employees who worry most about losing their jobs, since bad employees rarely recognize or admit their deficiencies.
- **Know what you want before you ask for it.** Vague questions produce vague answers. The more precise the request, the more likely people are to compile the information you need. A 50-page conglomeration of charts and figures fuels disorganization and clouds decisionmaking.
- **Collect and analyze data by team or department.** This sends the message "we're in this together" and tells everyone that responsibility for growth and improvement is shared. It also combats job isolation and promotes meaningful conversations among peers.

- **Avoid introducing high-stakes information prematurely.** If pressure is too high from the onset, employees are apt to shut down before the process is even under way. Also, short-term solutions—such as test prep—become the panacea, whereas long-term solutions such as improving teaching practices or aligning curriculum are completely overlooked. Try to assemble a coalition of supporters first before going right to the hammer.
- **Keep it simple.** The less complex the goal, the more likely people are to reach it. Devising an outcome that addresses a specific benchmark to reach over time is a good approach. For example, a simple goal might be to raise the percentage of schools making their Average Yearly Progress target or increase the number of completed work orders each month. Narrowing the focus by concentrating on a single mark sets staff up for a win.
- **Make the invisible visible.** People cannot change what they don't see. Patterns and deficiencies need to be revealed, especially because educators have a hard time making the connection between their efforts and accomplishments. Examining some of the less obvious sound bytes may actually lead to greater precision and accuracy.
- **Inundate practitioners with success stories.** Success stories motivate those who are already using data and squelch the histrionics of recalcitrant employees. It does not take much searching to find something positive to report. When teams are recognized for attaining goals in a results-driven context, they are energized to keep going.

Reliable and timely data force leaders to make tough choices, such as dropping a reading program that is not working or rethinking a long-standing practice that is nice to do, but not really necessary. They also promote inquiry-based discussions, lead to instructional fine-tuning, turn problems into opportunities, and give people cause for celebration. "Fresh data in the hands of thoughtful analysts and wise professionals is a pearl beyond price" (Doyle, 2003, p. 96). The challenges public schools face in using data are difficult, but not insurmountable. The time is ripe for educational leaders to clear the fields and plant the seeds for success.

CONCLUSION: IT'S ELEMENTARY

The fictional English detective Sherlock Holmes used his uncanny power of memory, observation, and logic to solve mysteries. When Holmes traveled to crime scenes, he tried to distinguish between what was incidental and what was vital. The Sherlockian way was to approach each case with a blank slate, to take notice of details that others failed to see, and to pursue contradictions to assumptions. By forging new insights, Holmes was able to draw conclusions that were often brilliant in their simplicity.

School leaders who find themselves overwhelmed by data can embrace the basic principles of this preeminent sleuth. For unpracticed users, it may seem daunting at first. But as meaningful information is relied on to approach problems, add or drop programs, or change ineffective routines, the process becomes contagious.

1. **Stick with the facts.** Avoid the temptation to form premature theories based on speculation or insufficient data. Otherwise, facts get twisted to suit theories instead of theories formulated to suit the facts.

2. **Don't be hasty.** Forging and testing every link in a chain leads to sound conclusions. Hasty decisions based on partial or faulty information can be disastrous.

3. **Put yourself in others' shoes.** Pay attention to how people perceive things to understand where they are coming from. Although two people may see exactly the same object, what is actually noticed might differ greatly. Be open to new ways of looking at a situation by putting yourself in others' shoes.

4. **Learn from your mistakes.** Do not be so overly confident that you forget reason. Whenever Holmes got overconfident, he told Dr. Watson to whisper "Norbury" into his ear. Norbury was one of the few cases where Holmes's investigative prowess went awry.

5. **Search for the truth.** A convincing body of evidence provides a higher probability of success. In the business of educating children, the truth is far better than infinite doubt or deception.

The average citizen believes that standards and testing guarantees learning for every student. Parents expect schools to be accountable for the academic achievement of their children. For these reasons, legislation such as NCLB and other sweeping reforms often pass with nary a whimper. Handwringing by superintendents, principals, teachers, or employee groups only polarizes the educational community and feeds into the draconian approach of policymakers who say schools are not doing enough to improve.

If educators do not get a solid grasp on data collection or they refuse to integrate available information into their decisionmaking, school systems remain vulnerable to external accountability measures. Rather than waiting for things to happen to them, sensible leaders make things happen for them as they strive for enduring greatness.

6 Is the Sky Really Falling?

Distinguishing a Bona Fide Crisis From Make-Believe

One person's emergency is another's minor annoyance.

—Mark McCormack (2000)

THE STORY OF URGENT ERNIE

Once upon a time, there lived a conscientious school safety coordinator named Urgent Ernie. Urgent Ernie prided himself on making sure bad things never happened.

One day as Ernie perused the latest Internet warnings on possible weapons of mass destruction hidden inside the lunchboxes of kindergartners, a ceiling tile fell onto his head. "The sky is falling," cried Ernie. "I must go and tell the superintendent."

As Urgent Ernie rushed to Headquarters, he ran into his friend Gloomy Doomay. "Good morning, Ernie," said Gloomy. "Where are you going?"

"Oh, Gloomy, the sky is falling!" said Urgent Ernie. "I must go and tell the superintendent."

"How do you know it's falling?" asked Gloomy.

"I saw it with my own eyes. I heard it with my own ears. And a piece of it actually fell on my head!" Ernie replied.

"I knew something bad would happen one day," lamented Gloomy. "I'll go with you so we can tell the superintendent together."

As they hurried along, Transportation Supervisor Emergencia drove up in her little yellow school bus. She poked her head out the window and called out, "Good morning, gentlemen. Where are you off to in such a hurry?"

"Oh, Emergencia," cried Gloomy. "The sky is falling. We must go and tell the superintendent."

"How do you know?" inquired Emergencia.

"Urgent Ernie told me," answered Gloomy. "In fact, he saw it with his own eyes, heard it with his own ears, and a piece of it actually fell onto his head."

"Hop on," said Emergencia. "This truly is an emergency. I'll turn on my flashing red lights and drive you to Headquarters, lickity-split."

As the bus approached the parking lot, they encountered Director Dependency talking on his two-way radio. "What's up?" Dependency asked.

"Oh, Director," exclaimed Emergencia. "The sky's falling and we have to tell the superintendent right away!"

"How do you know the sky's falling?" asked Mr. Dependency.

"Gloomy told me," said Emergencia.

"Urgent Ernie told me," Gloomy responded.

"I saw it with my own eyes. I heard it with my own ears. And a piece of it actually fell on my head!" squealed Ernie.

To which Director Dependency replied, "Oh my goodness! The superintendent is away at a conference. Who will tell us what to do? Let's drive along the interstate and try to find the superintendent. Without her, we really can't make a decision."

As Emergencia put the pedal to the metal, Dependency whipped out his electronic devices to text, beep, and buzz his trusty assistant, Ms. Catastrophe. Ms. Catastrophe was instructed to contact the highway patrol and request that a Superintendent Alert be posted on the freeway signs throughout the county. Ms. Catastrophe quickly complied, but not before running around the building and telling all the other assistants, "Get under your desks. The sky is falling!" When colleagues pressed for details, Ms. Catastrophe shouted, "Director Dependency saw it with his own eyes, heard it with his own ears, and a piece of it actually fell on his head." The assistants stopped answering telephones and tossed aside half-typed memos so they could crawl to safety.

Back on the interstate, traffic began piling up as vehicles slowed to read the Superintendent Alert and jot down the license plate number. It wasn't long before cars came to a complete standstill. Soon the surface streets became clogged as drivers exited the freeway to search for a less congested route. Within a few hours, the worst gridlock in the state's history had shut down the major transportation corridors within a hundred-mile radius. And smack-dab in the middle of it all sat the little yellow school bus with the entire district office staff huddled inside waiting for the sky to fall.

Meanwhile, back at Headquarters, the superintendent—who had decided to skip the conference—sat in her office reading e-mail and catching up on paperwork. She couldn't remember the last time her morning was so interruption-free. In fact, the superintendent thought it might be a good idea to schedule a lunch meeting with her management team, but learned they were all out of the office. It was just as well, since she could certainly use the time to catch up.

NO NEED TO "FUD" ABOUT IT

In the wake of senseless tragedies like Paducah, Columbine, and Red Lake, minimizing the importance of school safety is certainly not in anyone's best interest. Although these very real crises mark the extreme, security plans must nonetheless be beefed up to adapt to changing information and world events. Yet thankfully, schools across the United States remain some of the safest places on earth. To stay this way, suspicious activity and threats should be treated seriously without overreacting. Perpetuating needless anxiety is actually an occupational hazard. Although scare tactics may work at first, people eventually become numb to the falling-sky warnings. Before long, prevention is replaced by skepticism, and even the most basic tenets of caution are overlooked. This is actually more harmful than the Urgent Ernie Syndrome, since skepticism leads to a desensitized view of potential dangers and causes staff to let down their guard completely.

Thoughtful and balanced planning keeps an organization protected and prepared. As districts brace themselves for unanticipated emergencies, a range of responses should be calibrated according to the risk factors involved. Overdoing it with security is disruptive and feeds into what has been described as the FUD frenzy—fear, uncertainty, and doubt. Relying on sound intelligence instead of rumor and innuendo allows appropriate personnel to exercise vigilance without summoning the SWAT team whenever a piece of ceiling tile comes down.

Since every situation on a campus is certainly not a crisis, common sense goes a long way in turning ongoing "melodrama into mellow drama" (Carlson, 1997, p. 144). Activating Code Red time and time again spreads paranoia and minimizes the significance of good planning. For heaven sakes, the sky isn't falling. And even if it were, sensible leaders have viable plans to prop it back up safely.

FIGHTING THE ADRENALINE RUSH

In the frenetic pace of 21st-century living, small annoyances can easily manifest into epic events. Blowing things out of proportion not only makes people feel important, it feeds the adrenaline rush that many have come to depend on for energy and excitement. Despite the fact that an addiction to urgency is stressful, creates tension, and leads to exhaustion, it also makes individuals feel useful, successful, and validated (Covey, 1994).

Being busy and overworked is a bit of a status symbol among school leaders. It also provides a nice excuse for bypassing the most vital aspects of learning leadership. Concentrating on instructional issues takes in-depth conversations, reflection, and perseverance. Conversely, handling operational dilemmas gives one the feeling that something is actually get-ting accomplished. This fills a temporary void formed by other unmet needs. In the best-seller *First Things First*, Stephen Covey (1994) aptly described this phenomenon as he wrote: "Whenever there's trouble, we ride into town, pull out our six shooter, do the varmint in, blow the smoke off the gun barrel and ride into the sunset like a hero. It brings instant results and instant gratification" (p. 33). With so much going on through-out the school day, it is hard for leaders to distinguish between what's urgent and what's important.

Due to the hectic nature of their jobs, educational leaders have become quite adept at crisis management. A jolt of pleasure is actually experienced as they careen from one crisis to the next. Unfortunately, spending so much time on urgent issues leaves no time to consider if what is being done really warrants doing.

Does urgency seem to be overpowering your life? At work, are you constantly gearing up for an imminent attack of whatever? The adrenaline addiction predictors in Form 6.1 will assess your propensity to thrive on a whirlwind of chaos. For the true Urgentaholic, the only way to battle this nasty disease is a complete attitude overhaul. Failure to change the man-ner in which events are responded to leaves people immobilized by a slew of little things. This simply compounds frustrations and further hampers one's ability to do a good job.

A fixation on adrenaline is self-deceptive and establishes an irrational way of thinking. When compared to other compulsive disorders like substance abuse, gambling, eating, or shopping, a leader's obsession with urgency mirrors many of the same addictive patterns addressed in 12-step recovery programs. These universal characteristics include (Covey, 1994):

✓ Predicable, reliable sensations from the substance or activity.
✓ Being completely absorbed by the substance or activity.
✓ Temporary escape from pain, worry, or other troubles.
✓ False sense of self-worth, power, control, intimacy, or accomplishment.
✓ Magnification of the problems and feelings the substance or activ-ity seeks to remedy.
✓ Diminished functioning, lack of ambition, and loss of relationships.
✓ Preoccupation with finding gratification via the substance or activity regardless of the consequences.

Form 6.1 Adrenaline Addiction Predictors

Answer these 15 questions with a yes (Y) or no (N) response in the right-hand column to determine if adrenaline addiction is affecting your work or home life in an adverse way.

1. Do you feel like you do your best work under pressure?	
2. Do you find yourself getting impatient with people who work or move more slowly than you?	
3. Are you nervous or anxious when you are away from the office for more than a few minutes?	
4. Did you stop what you were doing more than twice today to respond to an emergency?	
5. When you are playing with your kids or out with friends, are you truly present instead of silently replaying a scene from the latest drama at work?	
6. Do you turn off your cell phone when you get home, when you go to the gym, or when you are out with friends and family?	
7. Do you have a reputation as the "go-to" person whenever there is a problem?	
8. Have you missed an important family event or been late for an appointment in the last two weeks because a crisis erupted at work?	
9. Do you crave a problem or emergency if you haven't encountered one for a few days?	
10. Are you having difficulty sleeping, or do you feel tired all the time?	
11. Do you eat lunch at your desk or skip lunch completely?	
12. Does it always feel as if you are rushing from one place to the next?	
13. Is it impossible to catch your breath before the next urgent situation or project emerges?	
14. Do you ignore people or push them away to finish an assignment?	
15. Have you taken a vacation in the past year?	
If you answered yes to any of these questions, consider it a warning sign that you may be predisposed toward an addiction to adrenaline. If you answered yes to any three questions, the chances are high that you're certifiably harried and urgency is your primary modus operandi. If you answered yes to four or more questions, you are definitely an adrenaline addict. It is time to sign up for a 12-step recovery program and develop a new mind-set.	

SOURCE: Adapted from Alcoholics Anonymous (n.d.); Covey (1994, pp. 33–34); Stack (2004).

Since addiction is a cyclical event, three principles should be embraced to put a little perspective back into the field of education. Fretting over minor incidents causes nervous agitation, impedes any chance for rational thinking, and decreases ambition. The power to put first things first is generated by finding pleasure in calm, focused activities rather than turning every mishap into a crisis.

1. Belabor Balance. When there is equilibrium between one's personal and professional life, it is easy to achieve inner peace. Getting regular exercise, eating sensibly, taking vacations, practicing the art of laughter, scheduling play dates with friends and family, and associating with positive people all translate into a healthy and harmonious existence. The best way to lower your stress quotient and move beyond survival mode is to renew your commitment to balance and moral purpose.

2. Determine Your "True North." Covey (1994) described this as defining where you are, where you hope to go, and how you want to get there. Without discernible goals that frame the future and build on the past, leaders may climb the ladder of success, only to discover that the ladder is propped against the wrong wall. Effective administrators know their true north and steer people in that direction with stoic resolve.

3. Shore Up Your Emotional Intelligence. Emotional intelligence is the capacity to recognize and monitor feelings and to use this information as a coping mechanism. The following components of emotional intelligence function as the preeminent barometer of effectiveness for school leaders, especially during turbulent times (Lovely, 2004):

A. *Self-Awareness.* The ability to examine one's own thinking, moods, and actions and understand the effects these responses have on others. By turning the mirror inward, school leaders can make choices to modify their temperament and style. As a result, their sphere of influence is enlarged significantly.

B. *Emotional Management.* An internal global positioning system that allows a person to recognize when he or she is mentally or physically off course. It tells individuals when they are behaving in a way that contradicts their principles and helps rechannel emotions to get back on track.

C. *Motivation.* The capacity to seize opportunities, transcend current circumstances, and rewrite the script when necessary. Since unforeseen events are going to occur in schools, leaders have to be flexible and prepared to face these events with courage, common sense, and optimism. Effective administrators recognize that gentle, relaxed people can still be superachievers.

D. *Empathy.* The ability to uplift the spirits of others without judging, mind reading, or problem solving. Empathetic administrators project acceptance and servitude toward those who may feel scared, dejected, or upset. True empathy requires genuine listening, keeping opinions to yourself, and avoiding the need to be right.

E. *Relational Management.* Understanding the emotional fibers that make up others and treating them accordingly. Through good communication and rapport building, leaders can create group harmony during a crisis. But if instability is a daily occurrence tension, mistrust and suspicion dominate the climate and relationships ultimately suffer.

In a perfect world, people would go about their day at a carefree pace, never experiencing distractions or other stress carriers. Traffic would move along nicely, there would never be a line at the post office, and a prime parking space would beckon on each trip to the mall. Yet in reality, no one can control all that happens in life. What can be controlled, however, is the manner in which we react to different episodes and how we choose to see our environment. Thus, it is emotionally prudent to submit to the fact that those who die with the most crises on their vitae don't win!

SCHOOL LEADERSHIP IS NOT AN EMERGENCY

Whether an emergency consists of an irate parent on the telephone, a student fight during lunchtime, a late school bus, or a broken-down Xerox machine, there is usually a discrepancy between one's perception of a situation and how others see that same situation. For example, a 9-1-1 from a frantic teacher trying to use the disabled copier minutes before her next class is certainly not a travesty for the well-organized secretary. Conversely, a verbally abusive parent in the front office is likely to ruffle the feathers of the secretary, but may be regarded as a minor inconvenience by the teacher the parent is demanding to see. And in the big scheme of things, a late school bus probably doesn't worry the superintendent much, but it can get a real rise out of an already edgy principal.

Quite frankly, a majority of school emergencies are nothing more than disruptive events that cause people to stray from their normal schedule or routines. Because school-related emergencies are subjective, it is important to let staff and parents know what constitutes a true emergency and what is nothing more than a hiccup on the day's radar screen (see sidebar: "What Constitutes a Bona Fide Emergency?").

What Constitutes a Bona Fide Emergency?

Only the unanticipated forces that have the potential to be life-threatening should be defined as actual emergencies. These include:

- ✓ Physical injuries that necessitate first aid or other medical attention.
- ✓ Accidents or natural disasters.
- ✓ Crimes or threats of violence that call for an immediate response or action.

SOURCE: McCormack (2000).

When a leader is unsure about how to respond to a given emergency, be it authentic or make-believe, the following tips should be used to determine proper action (McCormack, 2000):

1. Ask what will happen if you do nothing. If there isn't anything that you should or can do about a situation, especially if the outcome is predetermined, it is best to do nothing.

2. Determine whether the emergency adversely affects your reputation, business, or relationships. Although disagreements and confrontations are part of life, not every unpleasant exchange is an emergency. However, if a conflict or situation is likely to have an adverse affect on your reputation, business, or relationships, then don't ignore it. If it is not, leave well enough alone.

3. Decide how long the fallout will linger after a particular event. If you are late to the parent-teacher association meeting, some might question your promptness, but hopefully you won't lose your parent following. On the other hand, abruptly leaving a hysterical teacher in your office after a blowup with a colleague may jeopardize your relationships with staff. Before taking a giant risk, consider the ramifications of your actions.

4. Ascertain what sacrifices you will have to make if you handle this emergency. If you drop everything to dig through the trash dumpster looking for a lost retainer, some other important task is going to be overlooked. But if it is worth putting off something else to find the missing dental appliance and ease the fears of a distraught teenager or avoid an afterschool encounter with a less-than-happy parent, then it is worth taking the time to join the search party.

5. Get out quickly and back on track. After you have done everything that needs doing to get a crisis under control, don't hang around rehashing the event with others who were or weren't involved. The goal is to remedy the situation quickly so that things are running smoothly again. Sometimes leaders spend just a few minutes on an actual emergency and then hours recapping inconsequential details.

With such vast potential for mishaps inside schools, it is possible for superintendents, principals, and central office managers to spend every waking moment fretting over hundreds of things that might go wrong. Yet fixating on impending doom creates stressed-out subordinates who are so busy paying attention to the future, they completely forget about the here and now. Asking, "Is this predicament as urgent as so-and-so is making it out to be?" or "How much will this matter a year from now?" enables administrators to cut themselves a little slack. As well-trained professionals, it is perfectly acceptable to stop sweating all the small stuff. After all, school leadership is not an emergency!

THE THROES OF CODEPENDENCY

When unbridled chaos fills the corridors of a school or an entire district, the crippling effects of codependency set in. Codependency manifests from insecurity and confusion. In codependent environments, one's behavior is primarily determined by the actions of another. Superintendents in the throes of codependency answer to school boards who specialize in micromanagement. Principals in dependency-dominated cultures struggle to make decisions and wait for the central office to tell them what to do. Teachers in turn rely on their principals for direction, yet exhibit rigidity and suspicion toward any change. A permission-based culture allows both administrators and faculty to blame mistakes and deficiencies on the decisions of others (Lambert, 2003). In codependent systems, employees are consumed by emotional drama and constantly search for answers outside themselves to feel better.

When employees experience a loss of self or are enmeshed in dysfunctional relationships, they end up feeling detached and fatigued. To eclipse such unhealthy patterns, it is up to those in charge to break this negative cycle. The boxed text, "Putting an End to Codependency," illustrates some key lessons in leadership to combat this common malady. Keep in mind that when quick fixes are sought to solve every problem, or when a lone member of the organization harbors all the vital information, or if decisions are made by a select few, collaborative structures are impossible to cultivate.

Putting an End to Codependency

- Seek advice from a representative group of stakeholders including new and senior teachers, clerical personnel, custodians, parents, and so forth.
- Redirect permission seeking by asking: "What do you think is the right thing to do? Why is/isn't this a good idea?"
- Give people choices instead of automatically saying yes or no to every request.
- Use language like *us, we,* and *our* rather than *I, my,* and *them: Our* staff vs. *my* staff; It's up to *us* to make this better vs. *them* at the district office; *We* have a good plan, rather than *I* have *my* plan.
- Postpone making a decision when it is not an emergency. Tell staff: "I'd like more time to think about this" or "How about if you submit your proposal in writing so I have the chance to fully understand it?"
- Let others represent the school and also be in charge of meetings, assemblies, and events. Rotate the roles of leadership to encourage broad-based participation.
- Don't get carried away by the power of your position. Make it clear that you don't have all the answers.

SOURCE: Adapted from Lambert (2003, p. 49).

CONCLUSION: BLOW OUT THE CANDLES AND MOVE ON

Few will ever forget where they were the morning the Twin Towers came down. Nor is it possible to ignore the barometer of emotions—confusion, outrage, sorrow, fear—still lingering as a result of this horrific event. Yet on the fateful day of September 11, 2001, and in the ensuing months, one leader stood out among all others in providing comfort as the nation tried to cope with its losses. Rudolph Giuliani's calm reassurance stretched from sea to shining sea.

In the aftermath of the tragedy, Mayor Giuliani embraced survivors, grieved for lost loved ones, pushed to get business and commerce moving again, and even gave people permission to laugh. From *Saturday Night Live* to the World Series and every conceivable place in between, it was as if the mayor never slept. We trusted him, we listened to his voice of reason, and we knew he was experiencing as much if not more pain than the rest of us. Despite how people felt about Giuliani before September 11, few disagree that he took on an iconic significance after it. It was Mayor Giuliani who gave a shell-shocked nation the strength to blow out the memorial candles and move on.

There is no doubt that crises are real events that happen in schools. The pivotal role an educational leader plays in guiding employees through tumultuous times certainly cannot be underestimated. In fact, it has been said that a CEO becomes the "star witness in the court of public opinion" during a crisis—whether he or she likes it or not (Atkinson, 2002). Therefore, recovery and resiliency after a catastrophic event are personified in the way a manager performs in the line of fire.

To prepare for emergencies without compromising organizational integrity, compare the best practices of Mayor Giuliani to the derailment of others who were less than heroic. During the Exxon *Valdez* oil spill, for example, CEO Lee Raymond considered the media his enemy and made every attempt to be an ostrich (Atkinson, 2002). The arrogant "culture of supremacy" that plagued the Enron bunch prompted a bankruptcy beyond comprehension. And a seemingly innocuous break-in at the Democratic National Headquarters brought down a president. In each fatal handling of these situations, the leader showed terrible judgment and refused to deal with mistakes early and decisively. Downplaying a disaster or entering the Spin Zone once the ground has started to rumble causes problems to grow exponentially.

Dealing with an emergency can be a defining moment for a school leader. Such dilemmas are used as opportunities to portray oneself as a thoughtful communicator; to practice making quick, systematic assessments of a problem; to exercise legitimate power; to display courage in spite of fears; and to direct a group's response. Leaders who fail to maintain their composure under siege or remain invisible during a crisis put their own reputation and the reputation of their school district in jeopardy. There's a Japanese proverb that says that the reputation of a thousand years may be determined by the conduct of a single hour. Administrators who anticipate problems and speak first about bad news, instead of allowing rumors to spread, get high marks in emergency management. Keeping your wits about you during a disastrous episode proliferates balance and serenity in the life cycle of an organization.

Epilogue: Let the Odyssey Begin

Good leadership is like gravity. It's felt everywhere but little understood.

—Jim Bencivenga,
Editor, *Christian Science Monitor* (2002, p. 36)

BALANCE INSIDE DISEQUILIBRIUM

Although there are a number of defining qualities that support the elements of successful school leadership, the concept remains illusive for many practitioners. Under a chokehold of complexity, it is becoming increasingly more difficult for people to churn better instead of more. In an industry in which knowledge, information, and ambiguity flow like the forces of Niagara Falls, it is hard to selectively capture the purest drops and let the rest simply float by. Complicating matters is an ideological shift in public education from a more familiar emphasis on programs and curriculum to the somewhat alien focus on learning and accountability.

Since 1998, the McREL Institute in Aurora, Colorado, has been synthesizing the growing body of leadership-based research to pinpoint practices that when applied appropriately, act as a catalyst for achievement (Waters, Marzano, & McNulty, 2003). This balanced framework is grounded in the notion that good leaders not only know what to do, but are also able to distinguish when, how, and why to do it. The McREL study outlines 21 key functions that directly influence learning. A number of functions such as order, discipline, focus, flexibility, situational awareness, and communication can be fine-tuned by applying the techniques in *Setting Leadership Priorities*. Discovering the nexus between leadership behavior and student growth has opened the door to reconstitute the way administrators are groomed and supported.

The most sensible way to promote harmony in the schoolhouse is to sprinkle a little yin with a little yang. This Taoist concept hinges on the creation of balance among opposing forces. By eclipsing masculine temperament with feminine style, a leader knows when it's time to slug (yang) and when it's time to hug (yin), when it's best to decide (yang) and when it's best to let it ride (yin), and when to act macho (yang) versus when to act maestro (yin) (Ramsey, 2003). According to the ancient Chinese, the fusion of yin and yang provides people a sense of direction, which ultimately imposes balance inside disequilibrium.

COURTING SUCCESSORS

As the new science of educational leadership evolves, administrators should concentrate on charting their own legacy. To leave an indelible footprint, rules have to be rewritten in a way that redefines the workplace and fosters learning communities that have yet to be conceived. When leaders believe all will be well after a given crisis blows over, once the superintendent retires, or when a new "Governator" is elected, they are lured into a den of complacency. After all, the only real power for improvement and control lies within ourselves.

Another ingredient to forge a lasting impression is the relentless pursuit of every possible angle to create a synergistic workforce. A good team will beat a great player any day of the week. Thinking you are competent or capable enough to go it alone—or are expected to for that matter—is utterly foolish. Plus, the nice thing about teamwork is there is always someone on your side. Synergy comes from putting the best people in key positions, developing individual strengths, bringing talent to the surface, delegating responsibility, and then moving out of the way so that folks can do their job.

Finally, and perhaps most important, bringing along successors to take over after you are gone is the sign of a selfless leader. Those cultivated today will determine how a school district looks tomorrow. Courting people into leadership roles instead of waiting for them to volunteer is the best way to shore up the next generation. This doesn't mean seeking out individuals exactly like you, either. Incestuous hiring is unhealthy for any employer and leads to clonelike management teams with little vitality or spunk. Contrary to popular belief, when everyone thinks alike, agrees all the time, or is afraid to rattle cages, organizations stagnate or, even worse, develop mono-vision. "A balanced team needs members who will argue politely, disagree respectfully, and challenge ideas that need to be questioned," says La Grange, Illinois, superintendent Dennis Kelly (1999, p. 36).

Concentrate courtships on those with the highest potential and integrity. Promote people for what they can become, not for what they have been. And never settle for mediocrity.

PASS THE *MATE*

The rich traditions of ancient civilizations often transcend the barriers of ethnicity, class, and occupation. Consider the native Guarani of South America as a case in point. Although colonization created diverse economic, social, and political structures, the special ways of these indigenous people capture the essence of modern-day Argentina, Paraguay, and southern Brazil.

It began more than 600 years ago with a plant known as *yerba mate* (pronounced MAH-tay). The bittersweet sap from the dark green leaf, a relative of holly, was ground into tea. Pre-Columbian tribes imbibed *yerba mate* for health, vitality, and longevity. When the Jesuits arrived at the turn of the 16th century, they quickly caught on to the tea's full-bodied flavor and ability to remedy hunger, thirst, and fatigue. The liquid also offered the priests a mystical comfort during the solitude of their existence. Soon, *yerba mate* became an agricultural staple throughout the *misiones* province. By the time other Europeans migrated to the area, the soothing powers of mate were widely known. Today, *yerba mate* plantations dot the trademark red soil of this subtropical region.

More than a simple beverage, the consumption of *mate* is an elaborate ritual shared by friends, family, and coworkers. An informal etiquette governs how the brew is prepared and served. The *matero* (server) fills a hollow gourd with crushed, dried *yerba* before adding hot water. Always drinking first, the *matero* then passes the gourd clockwise. Each participant sucks the gourd dry before handing it back to the *matero* for a refill. This "drink of the gods" is ingested through a wooden or metal straw, called a *bombilla*, which strains the grassy mixture. Enjoying a round of *mate* with others—including sharing the same straw—creates a bond of acceptance and intimacy. People talk, laugh, and debate as they engage in this fraternal act. Whether strolling the boulevards of Buenos Aires, relaxing at a remote *estancia* outside Asuncion, or climbing the falls of Iguazu, foreigners are hard-pressed to encounter locals without their trusty thermos, carved-out gourds, and silver straws.

Traditional rituals like the preparation and consumption of *yerba mate* carry deep meaning, occur routinely, and symbolize what is valued and held dear to a society. According to Deal and Peterson (1999), these familiar experiences provide a vital link to the past, reinvigorate the present, and offer a welcome promissory note for a robust future. Parallel structures in school systems characterize how educational traditions are honored and preserved. Although rules, job descriptions, and policies may define what employees do, the unwritten rules, informalities, and rituals of an organization actually determine how people behave. Shaping the culture is a delicate but not impossible act.

To enrich an organization's cultural landscape, managers have to read between the lines. It is only through careful scrutiny and attention that the heart, soul, and vitality of an enterprise is uplifted. For educational leaders to become ROBUST cultural icons (see sidebar), they must be sure of themselves without being full of themselves, exude self-confidence without being self-centered, and walk with a steady stride instead of a haughty swagger (Ramsey, 2003).

The ROBUST Flavor of a Cultural Icon

Resilient: is able to bounce back from and successfully adapt to adversity; constructively handles dissent and disappointment; is willing to admit errors and learn from them

Optimistic: remains hopeful while openly confronting the brutal facts of current reality; focuses on what is right about his or her job rather than what is wrong about it

Bold: takes stock of where the organization is and galvanizes employees to realize the vision; is a spontaneous risk taker; is thick-skinned

Undeterred: is unaffected by previous mistakes or failures; is comfortable with criticism; is not easily discouraged

Sensible: is cognizant of others' perceptions and feelings; applies common sense, logic, and sound judgment to respond to situations and make decisions; refuses to overreact

Team Driven: places strong emphasis on creating cohesive adult relationships; knows when to go to the bench and call up the second string; rarely attempts to go it alone

---

IF AT FIRST YOU DON'T SUCCEED, TRY, TRY AGAIN

During the infancy of my principalship, I began most mornings at 5:00 A.M. with a brisk run followed by a 3,000-yard master's swim class. Pulling into the school parking lot with damp hair and bike atop the car (for a postworkday ride) was routine. Weekends were chalked full of longer runs, harder rides, and frigid ocean swims. Ironically, for all the miles logged, races entered, and periodic pieces of hardware brought home, I was never quite satisfied with my performance. At that point in time, accepting the fact that high-intensity training did not always equate to high-quality results wasn't in my repertoire.

Now a decade older, out of shape, and grateful just to be able to get out of bed in the morning, it is easy to reflect back on those days as a multisport athlete and realize that triathlons are the perfect metaphor for educational leadership. Instead of the swim-bike-run combination, administrators build fitness around the diametrically different events of learning-operations-relationships. A solid base is established first before longer durations or speed work are added. If participants try to do too much at once, results are short-lived and the chances of injury are high. Each season, further improvements are made to an individual's overall conditioning. Just as it can take years to build a world-class athlete, so it goes with building a world-class leader.

As is the case with triathlons, each facet of educational leadership is performed independently of the next; however, it is impossible to be a successful competitor without balancing the three disciplines. Spending all one's time on a single dimension while neglecting other parts of the triangle can cause a physical or mental breakdown that sets you back a lifetime.

Although learning-operations-relationships incorporate a host of skills, levels of intensity, and equipment, the three activities are easily mixed into a single sporting combination. For school leaders to develop the requisite strength, stamina, and speed, they simply have to cross train like a triathlete. Beginning with learning, the practices apt to have the greatest impact on student achievement must be properly identified. Appropriate techniques can then be selected to drive the order of change so that measurable improvements occur. Whether it is promoting staff cooperation, fostering shared beliefs, or keeping the attention on clear goals and desired outcomes, the best learning leaders understand and take seriously their role as change agents.

In the area of operations, standard procedures are necessary to ensure a work site runs efficiently. Without order and routines, mayhem lies in wait just below the surface. In poorly managed school settings, the smallest anomaly can quickly snowball. Avoiding an avalanche calls for educational leaders to minimize interruptions, protect teachers and students from unnecessary distractions, remove scheduling barriers, and make sure employees have access to the resources they need.

Finally, the attention leaders pay to their human capital is a far better yardstick of accomplishments than the number of degrees lining the wall, number of titles after a name, or size of a paycheck. Nothing good can come of the absence of positive relationships in a workplace. In study after study, employee performance, job satisfaction, and loyalty are directly linked to relationships with supervisors and coworkers. Leaders who go the extra mile are keenly aware that relationship building is not a spectator sport. Thus, they leave their mark by investing heavily in people one commitment at a time. What a boss intends to communicate is far less important than how it is communicated. No amount of Teflon coating can mask insincerity or indifference. In the area of interpersonal relations, the truth of the matter is we are how we are perceived.

While the sport of triathlon continues to become mainstream, the concept of quality training over quantity of training sessions serves as the mantra for endurance athletes. Whether competing in a short sprint, middle Olympic distance, or grueling Ironman, it is impossible to accelerate to the next level of fitness without a careful mixture of inspiration (staying motivated), dedication (goals that cause stretching, but not breaking), and celebration (enjoying and applauding accomplishments). Going full throttle all the time depletes reserves, overstresses ligaments, and is a one-way ticket to the medical tent.

If you desire to do things well instead of doing things hard, embrace the five steps to quality training in the following list. Developing optimal results through less effort creates a legacy that is worth writing home about.

1. **More doesn't make you better:** Lighter wheels, high-energy drinks, heart rate monitors, and summer swim camps are all valuable additions, but none have the long-term impact of training right. You can work out around the clock and still be spinning your wheels. When a point of no return is reached at the office, mistakes are inevitable. Before you can go faster, harder, or longer, you need a good, solid base.

2. **Break up your training:** Triathlon is the ideal sport for the millennium because it combines total fitness with variation. What better way to experience the great outdoors than a refreshing swim in a mountain lake, a bike ride that winds through pristine countryside, or running on trails with scenery impossible to see from the inside of a car window? Learn to appreciate changes in the biorhythms of work by doing things differently. Visit classrooms at random times of the day and in an opposite sequence from the usual. Enter the building from the back door so you can greet people you normally don't see in the morning. Leave the office for lunch. Spontaneity and change keep a mind and body fresh.

3. **Know the course:** Experienced triathletes never show up on race day without knowing the course. If it is impossible to swim, cycle, or run the

actual course prior to a race, they read about it online, study elevation maps, and talk to people familiar with the terrain. School leaders need to research which way the wind is blowing and be aware of any twists and turns along the route. Relying on past successes, taking people for granted, or underestimating the significance of minor details can lead to costly errors.

4. Rehearse your transitions: One of the biggest challenges for novice triathletes is mastering the swim-to-bike and bike-to-run changes quickly and efficiently. Poorly executed transitions waste precious time and energy. Proficiency in the transition area takes concentration, practice, and advance planning. Laying out gear in the right order, adroitly stripping off a wetsuit, scoping out the location of your bike rack, and zeroing in on the exits can save valuable seconds. Leaders should practice their transitions by moving from one job function to the next in a seamless, fluid motion. Being swift but accurate, defining time constraints, compartmentalizing tasks, and thinking ahead are all great ways to fight the clock.

5. Be careful not to bonk: When multisporters find themselves void of energy at the end of a long workout, they refer to this depletion as the "bonk." Bonking results from poor hydration, fatigue, overtraining, or improper pacing. It is easy to start out hard on a bike ride, for example, and forget you have 80 miles to go that day. School leaders need to remember that without adequate pacing, ample fuel consumption, and a well-planned taper (a gradual decrease in training as it gets closer to race day) before a major event, they'll bonk!

Educational leadership is a fast-paced and hectic endeavor; but a well-trained administrator competes in the daily events with a steady and quick mind, razor-sharp determination, and the ease of a winner. The finish line is just around the corner. Anyone is capable of making it across with a little preparation, perspiration, and perspective. If at first you don't succeed, try, try again. The goal is to be better tomorrow than you are today. And never lose sight of the fact that the alternative to progress and achievement is atrophy and decay.

JUST DO IT

Whether your odyssey is just beginning or you've been at it a long time, it is never too early or too late to make improvements. New tricks are learned by those with the gumption to just do it! Unless administrators break free of trying to manage everything on their own, they will never be able to fully attend to that which transpires between teachers and students, even though this is where the rubber meets the road. "Mr. McVicker's

Breakthrough" in the Story Board is proof positive that when the deck is reshuffled, routines shall change for the better.

STORY BOARD: MR. McVICKER'S BREAKTHROUGH

The Breakthrough Coach (http://www.the-breakthrough-coach.com) is a mechanism that allows principals to radically alter their perspective to concentrate on the instructional, as opposed to managerial, aspects of their work. Listen to how 20-year veteran principal, David McVicker has used the model to redefine his role and make the job seem a bit more doable:

The Breakthrough training has been helpful to me in three primary areas. First, my office manager and I meet daily for 10–25 minutes to review paperwork, mail, and schedules. This has been a huge boost in communication for the two of us. As my right hand, my assistant must know what I'm doing and how she can best support me. The only drawback is that she still has way too much on her plate. So now I am concentrating on getting her workload reduced. Both the office manager and secretary have viewing rights to my calendar, but only the office manager can add dates or schedule appointments.

Cleaning my office was a monumental second step. I dumped at least three or four garbage cans of recycled material from my office and cupboards. Although I still have a bit more to do, my workspace looks 100% better and no longer is filled with so many distractions. Without those pilings calling me, I feel more focused and don't spend as much time trying to figure out where to begin.

Finally, the scheduled days in the classrooms have been especially rewarding. Presently, I devote two days per week to visitations with students and teachers. I have asked staff to let me know what kind of feedback is most beneficial and am using their input to refine the instructional support I might offer. For years I've wanted to spend more time in the classrooms and even included this as part of my annual professional goals, but never could find a systematic way to make it a reality. Now it is! I'm far more in tune with staff issues and needs, can check more frequently on students, and am able to support the entire faculty with timely and regular feedback. This is really what the job is all about.

I still have days when everything goes to the dogs and the moon is full and people are just strange, but on the whole, I think the Breakthrough strategy has made a significant impact for me.

David McVicker, Principal
Emerald Heights Elementary School
Silverdale, Washington, and 2005 Washington
State Distinguished Principal of the Year

Each day in communities across America, someone stops smoking, starts training for a marathon, enters rehabilitation, or reaches the summit of a mountain they had not climbed before. As hokey as it sounds, positive thinking is powerful. If you don't believe it, look around at the people you respect and admire most. Chances are excellent that these individuals sip from a glass that is half full. If they didn't, you probably wouldn't think so highly of them.

If you yearn to experience the gravity of good leadership, the tools in Resource A, "Leadership Lessons in 30 Minutes or Less," can act as a launchpad. These instruments are designed to guide you toward that breakthrough you have been waiting for. Instant success provides the motivation to keep going and prompts additional changes that may serve as the turning point in your professional life. Blue skies are indeed ahead. Let the odyssey begin!

Resource A: Leadership Lessons in 30 Minutes or Less

T he following resources are intended to help readers implement effective activities in a short period of time—which is usually all that busy administrators have. These activities are specifically designed to nudge the learning culture in a positive direction and can be used in 30 minutes or less.

1. Getting Results With Time-Efficient Meetings: Adapted from Mike Schmoker's (1999) book *Results: The Key to Continuous Improvement*, this meeting outline is an excellent tool for solving a single issue or concern and achieving a short-term goal. The format keeps participants focused on the desired outcome, is solutions driven, and moves at a fast pace. A meeting such as this requires a good facilitator who understands the importance of following the agenda and moving people along. Topics that require in-depth discussions or a more thorough examination of data may still be introduced using this format, with the caveat that the time frame be extended beyond 30 minutes.

2. The Classroom Walk'bout: As busy administrators try to get into classrooms more often and see learning in action, it is important they have a means of recording their observations in an easy and focused way. Trying to remember what was seen or heard and later reflect on this information with a teacher is next to impossible. Immediate and timely feedback is an excellent way for site administrators to practice instructional leadership.

The Classroom Walk 'Bout was created by George Manthey, a former school principal and current Professional Learning Executive for the Association of California School Administrators (ACSA). The instrument is a Personal Digital Assistant–based data collection system that generates immediate reports for teachers. It is specifically designed for multiple, short, and regular classroom visits and helps answer five key questions during a walkthrough:

1. Are students on task?
2. To what degree are content standards being covered?
3. Are effective teaching practices being used?
4. Are a variety of instructional strategies integrated into the lesson?
5. Are the differing needs of students being met?

For more information or to purchase the product, contact George Manthey at ACSA at 650.259.3416 or gmanthey@acsa.org.

3. Passing Out Psychological Paychecks: 50 Ways to Recognize Employee Performance and Boost Morale: People are a school district's biggest asset. Without effective administrators, stellar teachers, good secretaries, hardworking custodians, careful crossing guards, and competent bus drivers, the needs of students, parents, and the community at large will not be adequately met. Good treatment of employees leads to similar treatment of customers.

Employees desire tangible proof that their employer notices what they do. Rewards and recognition are symbols that someone saw and cared. In addition, when individuals feel valued and appreciated, they take pride in their work and are willing to go the extra mile for the organization.

These *50 Ways to Recognize Employees and Boost Morale* offer no-or-low cost means for leaders at every level of your organization to highlight excellent performance and let team members know their contributions are both worthwhile and meaningful.

1. GETTING RESULTS WITH TIME-EFFICIENT MEETINGS

The following model is adapted from *Results: The Key to Continuous Improvement* by Mike Schmoker (1999). This format enables a team to have a productive meeting in about 30 minutes—which is often all the time available. It can be tailored to fit a group's specific purpose or goal.

Before the Meeting

- **Agenda**—Distribute the agenda to participants in advance of the meeting.
- **Recording Tools**—Have flip charts, a white board, or a computer ready to record brainstorming ideas.
- **Designated Tasks**—Appoint a timekeeper, recorder, and facilitator for the meeting.

During the Meeting (1 minute)

The team leader should establish and articulate the purpose of the meeting. The desired outcome must be specific, with the focus being an agreed-on goal.

Strategies That Worked (5 minutes)

The team leader gives each member a chance to offer evidence of a strategy that was effective in helping reach the goal since the last meeting. The emphasis here is to be concise. The facilitator may want to apply the "20-second rule" to each speaker to increase the amount of ideas generated. This can also heighten the energy level and enhance clarity of expression.

Chief Challenges (3–5 minutes)

Team members identify the most urgent concerns or obstacles to achieving the desired results.

Proposed Solutions (8–10 minutes)

Practical and concrete solutions to these problems are suggested.

Action Plan (10 minutes)

Decide which solutions might be best for the team to focus on between now and the next meeting. If agreement does not emerge quickly, rank-order voting can be used to narrow the focus. If appropriate, the team may need to determine and record the names of the people who are responsible for follow-up assignments prior to the next meeting.

After the Meeting

The team leader distributes a memo or e-mail documenting the team's focus between now and the next meeting. If a laptop is used to record the minutes, this summary can be distributed electronically.

Summary

This type of meeting enables every team member to quickly take advantage of a maximum number of concrete ideas. It also capitalizes on each member's acquired expertise around a clear goal and strategic focus. The meetings are efficient and results based.

SOURCE: Schmoker, M. (1999). *Results: The Key to Continuous Improvement*, pp. 119–120. Used with permission.

2. THE CLASSROOM WALK'BOUT

The Walk'bout™—Longhand Form

Start Time **Date** **Day of Week**

Teacher
 ☐ Monday
 ☐ Tuesday
School
 ☐ Wednesday
 ☐ Thursday
Subject
 ☐ Friday

Percent on Task **Grade Level** **Course**
☐ All
☐ Most **Period** **Room**
☐ Some
☐ Few
☐ None **Type of Classroom:** ☐ Regular Education ☐ Self-Contained EL
 ☐ Special Education ☐ Alternative
  Education

Student Activity

Depth ☐ Recall Level ☐ Strategic Thinking
 ☐ Skill/Concept Level ☐ Extended Thinking

Predominant Effective Practice
☐ Identifying similarities and differences
☐ Summarizing and note taking
☐ Reinforcing effort/providing
 recognition
☐ Homework and practice
☐ Representing knowledge
☐ Learning groups

☐ Setting objectives/providing feedback
☐ Generating and testing hypotheses
☐ Cues, questions, and advance
 organizers
☐ Other
☐ Not observed

Other Effective Practice

Effective Practices Also Used		*Instructional Mode*
Identify Similarities and Differences	☐ Yes	☐ Individual
Summarize and Take Notes	☐ Yes	☐ Small group
Reinforce Effort/Provide Recognition	☐ Yes	☐ Whole class
Homework and Practice	☐ yes	
Nonlinguistic Representations	☐ Yes	
Cooperative Learning Groups	☐ Yes	
Set Objectives/Provide Feedback	☐ Yes	
Generating and Testing Hypotheses	☐ Yes	
Cues, Questions, Advance Organizers	☐ Yes	

Page 1
a *Quality Solution* from *ACSA*

Teacher Activity
- ☐ Direct Instruction, Whole Group
- ☐ Direct Instruction, Small Group
- ☐ Individual Instruction
- ☐ Lecture
- ☐ Monitor/Provide Feedback
- ☐ Lead Discussion
- ☐ Film
- ☐ Test
- ☐ At Desk/Computer
- ☐ Attending to Misc. Needs
- ☐ Monitoring Transition

Checking for Understanding
- ☐ Presses On
- ☐ Reads Body Language
- ☐ Asks Clarifying Questions
- ☐ Polls
- ☐ n/a

Differentiated Instruction
- ☐ Not Obvious
- ☐ By Lrng Style
- ☐ By Ach Level
- ☐ By Style and Level
- ☐ n/a

Targeted Strategies

Differentiation by ELD Level	☐ Yes	☐ No	☐ n/a	☐ Not noted
Active Student Involvement	☐ Yes	☐ No	☐ n/a	☐ Not noted
Print-Rich Environment	☐ Yes	☐ No	☐ n/a	☐ Not noted
Access Prior Learning	☐ Yes	☐ No	☐ n/a	☐ Not noted
Social Interaction	☐ Yes	☐ No	☐ n/a	☐ Not noted
Objective Is Clear	☐ Yes	☐ No	☐ n/a	☐ Not noted
Verbal With Visuals	☐ Yes	☐ No	☐ n/a	☐ Not noted
Emphasize Key Vocabulary	☐ Yes	☐ No	☐ n/a	☐ Not noted
Use of Nonlinguistic Cues	☐ Yes	☐ No	☐ n/a	☐ Not noted
Wait Time	☐ Yes	☐ No	☐ n/a	☐ Not noted

Standards-Based Models of Student Work Are Visible and Discussed With Students

Standards and Rubrics Posted	☐ Yes
Standards-Based Student Work Posted	☐ Yes
Student Description of What Is Being Learned	☐ Yes
Students Explain Criteria Met by Work	☐ Yes

Comments

Observer

End Time

a *Quality Solution* from *ACSA*

3. PASSING OUT PSYCHOLOGICAL PAYCHECKS

50 Ways to Recognize Employee Performance and Boost Morale

If You Are a Superintendent

1. Nominate a principal or central office manager for an Outstanding Contributions to Education award.

2. Establish an Employee of the Month program for central office staff. Nominations can come from peers or supervisors. Hang the selected employee's picture in the lobby and provide him or her a special parking space next to yours.

3. Get into the trenches by riding a school bus to and from work, helping serve lunch in the high school cafeteria, or aiding in a special education class for a morning. This builds empathy and shows the value you place on positions that often go unnoticed.

4. Have the communications department make a promotional video profiling the people in your school district who make it such a great place to work.

5. Go on a listening tour to gather input about how to do things more efficiently or streamline operations. Implement employees' suggestions and give credit where credit is due.

6. Require every certificated administrator at the central office (including yourself) to substitute in a classroom one day per year.

7. After a school or classroom visit, send a handwritten thank-you note to the teacher or principal.

8. When you observe an employee providing great customer service, write a complimentary note on the back of a business card and hand it to the employee immediately.

9. When paychecks go out, write a few words on the envelope highlighting something spectacular you heard about that person during the month.

10. Create a yearbook to be displayed in your office or the front lobby containing photos of district staff members and their best achievement of the year.

If You Are a School Board Member

1. Read to students and donate the book to the classroom library. Provide a separate resource-type book for the teacher inscribed by you.

2. Speak to the high school Associated Student Body about school governance. Invite students to provide input about various board policies affecting them (dress code is sure to come up). Although their ideas cannot always be implemented, it gives trustees a chance to make direct contact with their customers. Follow up with a thank-you letter to the ASB advisor.

3. After attending athletic events, write a congratulatory note to the coach and team for "achieving victory with honor" or "giving it their all."

4. Nominate a member of the superintendent's cabinet for an Administrator of the Year award.

5. Send a note to principals after visiting their campus, attending a school event, or learning about a significant achievement.

6. Recognize performance of employees who are not usually in the limelight with a Behind the Scenes award at the beginning of every board meeting.

7. Give a monetary bonus to the schools with the best student attendance each semester. With the consent of the respective unions, do something similar for employee attendance.

8. Honor loyalty and longevity by creating a Decade of Helping Hands display on the outside wall of the central office. When employees reach 10 years of service in the district, they get to leave a pewter or ceramic handprint on the wall.

9. Deliver a fruit basket on behalf of the board to a school or department deserving of "fruitful" congratulations.

10. During the day or week of the administrator, cook breakfast for the entire management team or schedule a Saturday picnic at the park. Use personal (not district) funds to pay for this.

If You Are a Central Office Administrator

1. Allow employees to leave an hour early the day before a holiday.

2. In the fall, take your entire staff to Happy Hour to celebrate the successful opening of school. At the event, share an anecdote about how each individual helped get the year under way without a hitch.

3. Pass around a special trophy for people to display on their desks for stellar results achieved.

4. Schedule a day in honor of an employee (i.e., Susie Jones Day) by sending a flyer to the entire department that explains the reason

for the honor. Decorate the honoree's desk and invite the middle or high school choral group to provide a noontime serenade.

5. Start a Lunchtime Learning Club using short journal articles or assigned book chapters that inspire improvement or innovation in your department. Provide the lunch, but be sure everyone knows that participation is voluntary.

6. Give comp time to individuals who make a significant contribution to the department, especially during a crunch or after the completion of a major project.

7. Name a place around the office after an employee and put up a temporary sign (i.e., Bill Williams Walkway or Cindy Smith Lounge).

8. Select various staffers to accompany you on school visitations. Without putting anyone on the spot, solicit input about how your department (or this particular individual) has been helpful.

9. Have department shirts made for everyone. Allow staff to wear these shirts on special "team" days.

10. Send staff to training or conferences that provide topics of interest and support the department's mission.

If You Are a Principal

1. Invite an employee into your office just to say thank you, without discussing any other issue.

2. Write a letter to the superintendent complimenting a staff member for a job well done. Copy both to the employee and his or her personnel file.

3. Make a donation to a charity in an individual's or group's name to acknowledge a compassionate act.

4. Without being asked, have someone from risk management come out and inspect the ergonomic comfort of the clerical staff. If appropriate, surprise employees with new chairs. You can even make the furniture delivery ceremonious by tying the chairs with a big bow.

5. Designate two employees (one teaching, one nonteaching) as Awards Ambassadors to provide an extra set of eyes and ears about the type of recognition employees seem to value most. Ambassadors should be honest about which incentives are and are not working. These individuals are an excellent resource for broadening the spectrum of accolades.

6. Pass out lottery tickets or gift certificates to employees who make a suggestion that is used. Keep a stack of these in your drawer so they can be distributed right away.

7. Leave a handwritten note after an impromptu classroom walk-through that highlights a noteworthy teaching or learning activity you observed.

8. Leave a Good News phone message on an employee's answering machine complimenting him or her for something wonderful that was done that day. What a great surprise to come home to!

9. Teach a lesson for a class period and give the faculty member much needed release time. Keep Free Lesson Passes on hand to place in teachers' boxes as appropriate.

10. Form a Principal's Advisory Council with top performers. Heed their advice and acknowledge members publicly for their fabulous ideas. Responsibility and visibility are huge incentives.

If You Are a Coadministrator

1. When you hear a positive remark about an individual, seek that person out as soon as possible to repeat the compliment.

2. Send birthday cards to employees.

3. Make a digital movie profiling teachers "doing it right." Have a surprise premiere at a faculty meeting.

4. Cover a teacher's yard duty as an expression of gratitude after they have stepped up to the plate.

5. Put up a large piece of butcher paper in the staff lounge so employees can write Praise for Peers messages. This allows everyone in the building to disclose stories about the help and heroics of others.

6. Schedule a Daily Humor Break with clerical staff. Ask someone to tell a funny story or share an anecdote with the group.

7. Volunteer to do a classified employee's least desirable duty for an entire day.

8. On an employee's anniversary date of hire, surprise him or her with a rose.

9. Send a complimentary e-mail to a staff member and a copy to the principal.

10. Post a News Flash on the school marquee when employees reach a particular milestone (i.e., "Congratulations Ms. Jones for earning a master's degree"; "Hooray Coach Smith for your fifth consecutive championship!").

Resource B:
Sample Complaint Procedures

COMPLAINT PROCEDURES—BP 1312.1(a)

Capistrano Unified School District exists to provide the best educational program and learning environment possible for all students entrusted to its care. To that end, the district welcomes constructive criticism of policies, programs, or operational decisions to improve its efforts and be responsive to its clients. To the extent that the district might need to consider changing a current practice or revisit a previous decision, it endeavors to do so in a deliberate and orderly manner. The district also has a need and desire to protect its employees from frivolous complaints that could serve as distractions to the effective pursuit of the district's mission.

Students, parents/guardians, and community members within the district having a complaint or disagreement about an issue, situation, or employee decision or action and seeking a specific redress are asked to follow the procedures outlined in this policy to have the complaint, grievance, or difference of opinion addressed in an orderly manner. The procedures outlined herein are intended to be responsive yet fair, to encourage thoughtful deliberation, and to make clear a complainant's avenues of appeal.

In the interest of protecting the rights of anyone seeking redress of a perceived grievance, no harassment or retaliation of any kind against a student, parent/guardian, or community member shall occur because a complaint was filed.

It is the intent of the Board of Trustees that matters giving rise to a complaint be addressed first on an informal basis and at the level closest to the situation. If a complaint cannot be addressed and resolved informally, then the formal steps of Levels 2, 3, and 4 are available to any complainant leading, if necessary, to ultimate resolution by the Board of Trustees.

If a complaint by a parent concerns review and changing of a student's written record, including the student's grade(s), this policy shall be superceded by the protocol spelled out in Education Code Sections 49070 and 49071.

If confidentiality is a concern, every effort shall be made to respect the wishes of the complainant, without compromising the rights of all other parties involved.

I. Level 1 (Informal Level)

a. In an effort to seek immediate resolution of the concern, the complainant shall first interact with the individual who is the subject of the complaint or is in the best position to address the complaint if it is a non-personnel-related matter. The only exception shall be if a situation exists that is determined to be extremely sensitive or that could represent a violation of law or district policies.

b. If the complaint is not resolved at the direct contact level, the complainant shall confer with the immediate supervisor of the employee who is the subject of the complaint or who is in the best position to take action on a non-personnel-related complaint. The supervisor shall communicate with the employee who is the subject of or closest to the complaint, and any other involved parties, in an attempt to assist in informally resolving the issue. Until such informal communication with the employee and employee's supervisor has been completed, the complaint shall not progress to the formal procedure outlined in Level 2.

c. If the supervisor of the employee who is the subject of the complaint (or the person in the best position to address a non-personnel-related complaint) is not able to satisfy the complainant, the supervisor shall make a decision either to find no cause to overrule the employee's decision or action, or on the other hand, to overrule the employee and then, through delegated authority from the superintendent, direct alternative action. The supervisor shall advise all parties of his or her judgment.

d. If the complainant is not satisfied with the outcome and chooses to pursue resolution to his or her personal satisfaction, the complainant may proceed to Level 2.

COMPLAINT PROCEDURES—BP 1312.1 (b)

II. Level 2

a. The complainant shall obtain, complete and submit a complaint form to the principal or appropriate department head. (Complaint forms, along with copies of this policy, are available at each school and the receptionist's desk in the district office, and can also be accessed on the district's website.)

b. The principal or department head shall review the completed complaint form and provide a copy to the employee who is the subject of the complaint (or in a position to resolve the complaint) and other involved parties, as he or she deems appropriate.

c. The principal or department head shall investigate the facts and, in a timely manner, communicate with the complainant, the employee who is the subject of the complaint, and others as he or she deems appropriate. He or she shall advise all parties of his or her decision either to find no cause to overrule the employee's decision or to overrule the employee who is the subject of the complaint and then, through delegated authority from the superintendent, direct alternative action. The principal or department head shall then advise all parties of his or her judgment.

d. If the complainant is satisfied with the principal's or department head's decision at Level 2, the completed complaint form shall be filed in the office of the principal or department head. If the complainant is not satisfied with the outcome at Level 2 and chooses to pursue further action, a copy of the completed complaint form shall be forwarded to the superintendent's office for processing at Level 3.

III. Level 3

a. The principal or department head, on notice from the complainant that he or she is appealing to Level 3, shall forward a copy of the complaint form to the superintendent's office. The principal or department head shall have completed that portion of the form reporting the disposition of the complaint, including a brief statement explaining his or her judgment regarding its disposition.

b. On review, the superintendent or designee shall, in a timely manner, issue a judgment regarding the complaint or, as an alternative, the superintendent or designee may forward the entire matter to the complaint review panel for an advisory opinion. The complaint review panel shall be composed of a parent, a school district employee, and a citizen representative appointed by the superintendent or designee.

c. Where the superintendent or designee has requested an advisory opinion from the complaint review panel, the panel shall conduct, in a timely manner, a hearing at which the complainant may present his or her case.

d. The complaint review panel, within five (5) working days of the hearing, shall render an advisory recommendation to the superintendent or designee. The superintendent, within five (5) working days of the complaint review panel's advisory recommendation, shall advise all parties of his or her final judgment.

e. If the complaint is not resolved to the personal satisfaction of the complainant after notification of the judgment by the superintendent or designee at Level 3, the final level of appeal shall rest with the Board of Trustees.

IV. **Level 4**

a. If the complainant wishes to appeal to Level 4, he or she must, in writing, request an appearance at a regularly scheduled meeting of the Board of Trustees where he or she shall be heard in accordance with Board Bylaw 9322 and the California Brown Act (EC54957). The board has the option to:

1. Take no action, which has the effect of upholding staff's earlier judgments.

2. Take action reversing staff's decision.

3. Take action modifying the direction of staff's decision.

b. The decision of the Board of Trustees shall be final.

Resource C: Testing Your Organizational DNA

How good are you at setting priorities—and sticking to them? What kind of genetic coding forms the nucleus of your management systems and routines? To test your organizational DNA, complete the questionnaire by indicating the degree to which each statement reflects your current behavior, patterns, and traits. If the statement *never* applies to you, circle 1. If it *always* applies to you, circle 5. If you do something once in a while, circle the number that best reflects how often.

1. If you made a list of what you want to do in an average week—work, spend time with family and friends, partake in a hobby—and another list of what you really do each week, the two lists would be almost identical.

NEVER   1   2   3   4   5   **ALWAYS**

2. You carry an organizational tool such as a day planner, Personal Digital Assistant, or notepad with you at all times.

NEVER   1   2   3   4   5   **ALWAYS**

3. If you were hit by a truck this afternoon, your family would know all the critical information necessary and would be able to find all the documents needed to carry on.

NEVER   1   2   3   4   5   **ALWAYS**

4. Your to-do list is a mile long. You could delegate something to your secretary, but you fret that she won't do it as well as you. You dare to delegate anyway.

NEVER   1   2   3   4   5   **ALWAYS**

5. When tasks become unmanageable, you break them into bite-size pieces so you aren't overwhelmed.

NEVER   1   2   3   4   5   **ALWAYS**

6. You pay attention to your biological clock by completing the most important activities of the day when you are at your prime.

NEVER   1   2   3   4   5   **ALWAYS**

7. You know exactly what you'll be doing at 9:30 A.M. tomorrow.

NEVER   1   2   3   4   5   **ALWAYS**

8. The parent-teacher association president (and best friend of a board member) asks you to help her out. Since you really don't have time this week, you decline the request and refer her to someone else for assistance.

NEVER   1   2   3   4   5   **ALWAYS**

9. You leave plenty of white space on your calendar to deal with interruptions and unanticipated events.

NEVER   1   2   3   4   5   **ALWAYS**

10. You ask for help—at home, at work—whenever you need it.

NEVER   1   2   3   4   5   **ALWAYS**

11. You schedule time for vital activities: paying the bills, getting medical checkups, and exercise.

NEVER   1   2   3   4   5   **ALWAYS**

12. You have cleaned out your closets or garage at least once in the past year.

NEVER   1   2   3   4   5   **ALWAYS**

13. There are no piles of unread journals, newspapers, or clutter lying around your office or home.

NEVER   1   2   3   4   5   **ALWAYS**

14. When worry becomes a problem, you act on it rather than let it intrude on your performance.

NEVER   1   2   3   4   5   **ALWAYS**

15. You answer e-mails and return phone calls at select times of the day.

NEVER   1   2   3   4   5   **ALWAYS**

16. You rarely (if ever) misplace things—car keys, documents, or other items of importance.

NEVER   1   2   3   4   5   **ALWAYS**

17. When an important project needs to be done, you are able to shut out distractions by closing your door.

NEVER   1   2   3   4   5   **ALWAYS**

18. You never give 100% to a project when 90% is sufficient.

NEVER   1   2   3   4   5   **ALWAYS**

19. If you grant an hour of your time to someone, you stick to your schedule. If the person arrives 20 minutes late, the meeting becomes a 40-minute affair.

NEVER   1   2   3   4   5   **ALWAYS**

20. You enjoy your job and know exactly why you chose the career path you did.

NEVER   1   2   3   4   5   **ALWAYS**

Scoring: Add all your points to determine your current level of organizational fitness.

SOURCE: Adapted from Stack, l. (2004). "Get Home Sooner." *Working Mother Magazine.* Working Mother Media Inc., and McCormack, M. (2002). *Getting results for dummies.* San Francisco: IDG Books.

90 or More: A Fine Molecular Specimen

Congratulations! You are an organized specimen and have little trouble completing tasks or staying focused. You understand what really matters and your goals remain a priority even when distractions are imminent. You are probably healthier and happier than others in your field of work.

80–89: A Chemically Balanced Organism

You have some good systems in place and stick to those systems most of the time. You understand the basic tenets of time management, order, and self-discipline. With a little-fine tuning, you can reach new levels of organizational prowess in your personal and professional life.

70–79: A Chromosomal Misfit

Sure, you are juggling several projects at once and people are coming at you from all sides, but the fact of the matter is you are disorganized. Try as you might, circumstances overwhelm you and you're out of sync with reality. You delude yourself with statements like "I thrive on chaos" or "I'll remember that." Stop pretending that tomorrow is going to be any better. Instead, make a commitment to break the cycle of bad habits by setting limited goals for improvement. Start by picking one day a week to leave the office an hour earlier.

Less Than 70: Genetically Defective

It may be a painful pill to swallow, but you're a mess. Life at home and work is an ongoing struggle. You constantly blame others for your troubles and make excuses for your lack of efficiency. You are chronically late for appointments and those who depend on you often feel let down. Procrastination and overload continue to mutate into more and more defective genes. If you don't alter your genetic makeup soon, you'll self-destruct. Find a coach or mentor to help you begin the reengineering process.

Resource D: Who Is Riding Our Bus?

PERSONAL INVENTORY

Directions: Put an X next to the word or phrase in each box that best describes you in your work environment. There are no right or wrong answers.

1.	2.	3.	4.
a. ____ Uncertain	a. ____ Timid	a. ____ Careful	a. ____ Principled
b. ____ Adventurous	b. ____ Impulsive	b. ____ Enthusiastic	b. ____ Warm
c. ____ Idealistic	c. ____ Submissive	c. ____ Sympathetic	c. ____ Loyal
d. ____ Self-assured	d. ____ Authoritative	d. ____ Dependable	d. ____ Hardworking
5.	**6.**	**7.**	**8.**
a. ____ Cautious	a. ____ Authentic	a. ____ Restrained	a. ____ Nonchalant
b. ____ Playful	b. ____ Popular	b. ____ Sociable	b. ____ Lighthearted
c. ____ Steady	c. ____ Neighborly	c. ____ Reliable	c. ____ Content
d. ____ Decisive	d. ____ Faithful	d. ____ Assertive	d. ____ Risk taker
9.	**10.**	**11.**	**12.**
a. ____ Logical	a. ____ Diplomatic	a. ____ Tactful	a. ____ Honest
b. ____ Carefree	b. ____ Jovial	b. ____ Talkative	b. ____ Confident
c. ____ Predictable	c. ____ Considerate	c. ____ Modest	c. ____ Eager to please
d. ____ Sensible	d. ____ Positive	d. ____ Outspoken	d. ____ Caring
13.	**14.**	**15.**	**16.**
a. ____ Humble	a. ____ Fair	a. ____ Fussy	a. ____ Accurate
b. ____ Expressive	b. ____ Imaginative	b. ____ Fun-loving	b. ____ Charming
c. ____ Satisfied	c. ____ Efficient	c. ____ People centered	c. ____ Adaptable
d. ____ Bold	d. ____ Thorough	d. ____ Results oriented	d. ____ Persuasive
17.	**18.**	**19.**	**20.**
a. ____ Curious	a. ____ Just	a. ____ Nonconformist	a. ____ Conventional
b. ____ Lively	b. ____ Optimistic	b. ____ Trusting	b. ____ Admirable
c. ____ Sincere	c. ____ Gentle	c. ____ Obedient	c. ____ Sensitive
d. ____ Productive	d. ____ Stable	d. ____ Self-reliant	d. ____ Competitive

SOURCE: Adapted from Lowry (1992).

NOTE: Personal survey available at http://evonneweinhaus.com/survey.htm.

Personal Profile Summary

Add up your responses in each category (*a, b, c,* or *d*) and record the totals below. Each letter is worth one point. Circle your highest score. This represents the primary style you display most often in the workplace. The second-highest score is your backup style.

Analyzer	Builder	Collaborator	Driver
a. _____	b. _____	c. _____	d. _____

Once your scores are tabulated, read the style descriptors below. For a staff to analyze its findings together and optimize team performance, use the Who Is Riding Our Bus? activity on the following page.

Style Descriptors

Analyzer (The Technician): Analyzers seek facts, prefer order, and are not afraid to challenge the logic of things. As independent thinkers, they are willing to disagree with the group leader. Analyzers excel at mining data. By exploring new concepts, they are able to build systems and create models that satisfy organizational needs. Most people appreciate the value of an analyzer's intellect, accuracy, and morals, but feel that sometimes they don't know when to back off or move on. At times, analyzers are seen as perfectionists and overly cautious because they don't like to be wrong. People describe analyzers as inventive, global thinkers, ethical, conventional, and candid.

Builder (The Harmonizer): Builders are goal oriented and believe the team's vision is important, yet are flexible and open to new ways of doing business. As troubleshooters, they are comfortable working outside defined roles and providing creative solutions to the group. Builders rely on their charm, optimism, and wit to influence others, which makes them excel at selling and promoting concepts. At times, however, builders neglect to put enough effort into a task or consider the needs of teammates. Because they don't like to be bogged down by details, they constantly search for shortcuts. This lack of discipline can exasperate colleagues. People describe builders as pioneers, natural storytellers, impulsive, jovial, and confident.

Collaborator (The Gatekeeper): Collaborators are process-oriented team players and seek areas of agreement. As respectful listeners, they strive to facilitate involvement, build consensus, and promote group stability— all in a relaxed atmosphere. Collaborators value their personal and professional relationships with others. However, their unhurried style can be frustrating to those who prefer structure and results. After all, their focus is on process, *not* product. Collaborators tend to shy away from confrontation and conflict. Such avoidance may lead to bigger problems later. People describe collaborators as adaptable, patient, considerate, relaxed, and good-natured.

Driver (The Backbone): Drivers are achievement-oriented individuals who like to lead. They enjoy risks and try to push a group to set high standards by providing a sense of safety and security. Drivers are dependable, are punctual, and come to meetings prepared to solve problems. However, their focus on completing tasks may come at the expense of maintaining a positive team climate. Their competitive nature can also make others uncomfortable. Because drivers thrive on being busy and efficient, they need to develop a little more patience, humility, and interdependence. People describe drivers as steadfast, responsible, practical, persistent, and dedicated.

TEAM ACTIVITY

Who Is Riding Our Bus?
Total Time: 30–40 minutes

Assessing Group Profiles (11–15 minutes): Once team members have completed their personal inventory and read the style descriptors, ask them to form like groups (i.e., all the drivers together, all the analyzers, and so on). Each team should respond to the following questions. A recorder can list the team responses on chart paper:

1. *What do you like about working with others who have the same primary style as your own?*

2. *What frustrates you about working with others who have a different profile or primary style?*

Share-Out (8–10 Minutes): Have a reporter from each group share his or her team's responses to the two questions. Although this will generate plenty of laughter, it also allows people to openly discuss their preferred style of play and lets others know what bothers them when they work on a team. Raising awareness of our wants and needs in a lighthearted, safe manner nudges group culture in a positive direction.

Wisdom Walk (3–5 minutes): At the conclusion of the share-out, pose the following questions to the group: "What would happen if our workplace was made up of only drivers? How might our school or department look if we were all collaborators?" and so forth.

Key points of emphasis for learning are:

- ✓ If an entire team or department is exactly alike, there will be a huge void in what can be accomplished at a work site.
- ✓ Knowing the "primary colors" of others raises awareness and breeds understanding. This is key to building successful team relationships.
- ✓ Although people may rely on a particular style most often, everyone is capable of altering his or her approach depending on his or her role at the moment.
- ✓ The most effective collaboration occurs when team members rely on their talents and inner resources to move in and out of different modes as needed.
- ✓ Without a blend of styles, a team will struggle with task attainment, lack creativity, encounter a higher degree of unstable relationships, and experience greater difficulty in achieving results.

Optional Pair Share (3 minutes): Find someone in the room who has a different profile than your own. Discuss any insights you gained about his or her preferred style through this exercise.

Self-Reflection: Where Do I Go From Here? (5–7 minutes): Review the reference guide for improved team relationships on the following page. Take a minute to think about how you might modify your behavior when working with a particular teammate to improve productivity or relationships. Write this down on a 3×5 card and take it with you. The goal is that the next time you come together to consult about a project or problem, you will have a better understanding of one another.

REFERENCE GUIDE FOR IMPROVED TEAM RELATIONSHIPS

To learn more about how you might enhance relationships with team members, locate your primary style along the top of the matrix. Then move down the left-hand column to find the primary style of a peer, subordinate, or supervisor. The suggestion box offers strategies for improving communication and interactions with colleagues.

You

Others	Driver	Builder	Collaborator	Analyzer
	The Backbone	The Harmonizer	The Gatekeeper	The Technician
Driver	Agree in advance on goals; identify shared responsibility; provide freedom to work within agreed-on limits; take turns being in charge.	Be honest; back up ideas with results; stick to agreements; acknowledge how completed tasks affect others' well-being; allow them to do things their own way.	Be businesslike; make them feel useful; allow them to make decisions; stick to the agenda; don't insist on a personal relationship.	Summarize facts; note accuracy and efficiency in their performance; let them decide how to approach tasks; recognize tangible results; allow them to focus on details.
Builder	Be more open about self and emotions; lighten up on time restraints; give them recognition; vary their roles and duties; let them learn by doing; provide on-the-spot assignments.	Let them take shortcuts if appropriate; reward their creativity; provide direction for reaching goals; assign them to teams in need of motivation.	Ask them for help in establishing short-term goals; provide clarity and focus; look for opportunities to be spontaneous; feed their ego by giving them a stage.	Spend time with them informally; promote their good ideas; recognize their need for excitement; quicken the pace; take a few risks with them.
Collaborator	Show personal concern for them and their family; provide timely and favorable feedback; give tangible rewards and recognition; seek their assistance in working with troubled employees.	Slow down your pace and volume; focus on one project at a time; when appropriate, involve them in unstructured, democratic settings; ask them for their suggestions; listen more.	Be strong, insistent, and direct; ask them to help you resolve conflicts; identify solutions jointly; respond to their honesty and sincerity in a like manner; build rapport.	Focus on their performance over the finished product; try to establish a personal relationship; encourage them to stretch their goals; ask them to be the spokesperson for the group.
Analyzer	Use facts and logic; recognize their knowledge and ingenuity; be patient while they evaluate things; give them a structure to follow; delegate projects that require technical solutions and allow plenty of latitude.	Talk facts, not opinions, and back them up with evidence; be patient; give positive feedback about their competence on a subject; don't force them to abandon tradition.	Show that you are technically competent; have them present data to the group; be firm when challenged; help them save face when wrong; let them build systems and leave the details to the drivers.	Don't apply undue pressure; provide perspective on solutions being considered; don't spend hours trying to prove your point if disagreement arises; divide and conquer the data logically.

References

Alcoholics Anonymous. (n.d.) *The 20 questions of Alcoholics Anonymous.* Available from http://members.ii.net.au~essbee/aa-wa/20%20questions.htm

Anderson, D. (2004, August 13). *Burden of data collection compromise schools.* Available from http://www.bizjournal.com/atlanta/stories/2004/08/16editoria14.html

Argyris, C., & Schön, D. (1974). *Theory in practice: Increasing professional effectiveness.* San Francisco: Jossey-Bass.

Atkinson, S. (2002, March 22). *A CEO's leadership is defined by crisis management.* Available from http://www.bizjournals.com/nashville/stories/2002/03/25/smallb5.html

Barth, R. (2002, May). The culture builder. *Educational Leadership, 59*(8), 6–11.

Bencivenga, J. (2002, February). John Kotter on leadership, management and change. *School Administrator, 59*(2), 36–40.

Blaydes, J. (1998). *The principal's book of inspirational quotes.* Brea, CA: Principal Publications.

Bridges, W. (1991). *Managing transitions.* Reading, MA: Addison-Wesley.

Carlson, R. (1997). *Don't sweat the small stuff . . . and it's all small stuff.* New York: Hyperion Press.

Center for the Future of Teaching and Learning. (2003). *The status of the teaching profession 2003.* Available from http//www.cftl.org/documents/CFTL2003 Powerpoint.pdf

Collins, J. (2001). *Good to great.* New York: HarperCollins.

Consortium on Productivity in Schools. (1995). *Using what we have to get the schools we need: A productivity focus for American education.* Available from http://www.ballfoundation.org/ei/research/using-print.html

Copland, M. (2001, March). The myth of the superprincipal. *Phi Delta Kappan, 82*(7), 528–533.

Covey, S. (1994). *First things first.* New York: Simon & Schuster.

CSR Research Consortium. (2002, June). *Evidence inconclusive that California's class size reduction program improves student achievement.* Available from http//www.classize.org/press/index-02.htm

Deal, T., & Peterson, K. (1999). *Shaping school culture: The heart of leadership.* San Francisco: Jossey-Bass.

DeMarco, T. (2002, September). Going paperless at board meetings. *School Administrator, 59*(8), 55.

Doyle, D. (2003, November). The new world of information technology. *Educational Leadership, 61*(3), 96.

Drucker, P. (1994, November). The age of social transformation. *Atlantic Monthly, 274*(5), 53–80.

Dufour, R., & Eaker, R. (1998). *Professional learning communities at work: Best practices for enhancing student achievement.* Bloomington, IN: National Educational Service.

Fullan, M. (1993). *Change forces: Probing the depths of educational reform.* Bristol, PA: Falmer Press.

Golemen, D. (1995). *Emotional intelligence.* New York: Bantam Books.

Hammonds, K. (2000, May). *You can do anything—but not everything.* Available from http://www.fastcompany.com/online/34/allen.html

Hargreaves, A., & Fullan, M. (1998). *What's worth fighting for out there?* New York: Teachers College Press.

Hargrove, R. (1999). *Masterful coaching.* San Francisco: Jossey-Bass/Pfieffer.

Heylighen, F. (1998, March 23). *Technological acceleration.* Available from: http://pespmc1.vub.ac.be/TECACCEL.html

Heylighen, F. (1999, February 19). *Change and information overload: Negative effects.* Available from http://pespmc1.vub.ac.be/CHINNEG.html

Holcomb, E. (2004). *Getting excited about data: How to combine people, passion and proof* (2nd ed.). Thousand Oaks, CA: Corwin.

Intermountain Center for Educational Effectiveness. (2001, April). *Effective schools process model.* Available from http://icee.isu.edu/EffectiveSchoolsModel.pdf

Kaser, J., Mundry, S., Stiles, K. E., & Horsley, S. (in press). *Leading every day: 124 actions for effective leadership,* 2nd ed. Thousand Oaks, CA: Corwin.

Kelly, D. (1999). *Lessons learned along the way: Survival tips for school leaders.* Arlington, VA: AASA.

Kouzes, J., & Posner, B. (1987). *The leadership challenge.* San Francisco: Jossey-Bass.

Lambert, L. (2003). *Leadership capacity for lasting school improvement.* Alexandria, VA: ASCD.

Leithwood, K., Louis, K., Anderson, S., & Wahlstrom, K. (2004). *How leadership influences student learning.* Minneapolis: University of Minnesota & University of Toronto, Ontario, Canada.

Lemley, R., Howe, M., & Beers, D. (1997). The new principal: Formulas for success. In *Quality School Leaders Series* (p. 52). Leadership Training Associates.

Lencioni, P. (2004). *Death by meeting.* San Francisco: Jossey-Bass.

Lovely, S. (2004). *Staffing the principalship: Finding, coaching and mentoring school leaders.* Alexandria, VA: ASCD.

Lowry, D. (1992). *True colors: Keys to personal success.* San Jose, CA: Communications Company International & the California School Employees Association.

Marzano, R. (2003). *What works in schools: Translating research into action.* Alexandria, VA: ASCD.

Mason, S. (2002, April). *Turning data into knowledge: Lessons from six Milwaukee public schools.* Available from www.wcer.wisc.edu/mps/AERA2002/Mason%20

McCormack, M. (2000). *Getting results for dummies.* Foster City, CA: IDG Books.

Murray, B. (1998, March). Data smog: Newest culprit in brain drain. *APA Monitor, 29*(3), 1–4.

Nelson, B. (1994). *1001 ways to reward employees.* New York: Workman.

Nelson, B. (1997). *1001 ways to energize employees.* New York: Workman.

Nicols, B., & Singer, K. (2000, February). Developing data mentors. *Educational Leadership, 57*(5), 34–37.

Pepperl, J., & Lezotte, L. (2004). *What effective schools research says: Instructional leadership.* Okemos, MI: Effective Schools Products.

Prochaska-Cue, K. (1995, July). *Thirteen timely tips for more effective personal time management.* Available from http://www.ianr.unl.edu/pubs/homemgt/nf172.htm

Pruitt, L. (2003, Fall). From a new principal's perspective. *New Teacher Center Reflections, 6*(3), 11, 15.

Queen, J. A. (2004, March/April). Desktop yoga: A stress suppressant. *Principal Magazine 83*(4), 45–48.

Ramsey, R. (2003). *School leadership from A–Z.* Thousand Oaks, CA: Corwin.

Reeves, D. (2004). *Assessing educational leaders.* Thousand Oaks, CA: Corwin.

Robbins, P. (2004, November 4). *Shaping positive and transforming toxic cultures.* Workshop presented at the Association of California School Administrators Annual Conference, San Diego, CA.

Robertson, P. (1999, February). *Time management practices of school principals in the United States.* Available from http://scholar.lib.vt.edu/theses/available/etd-042199–205455/unrestricted/TITLE.PDF

Sage Learning Systems. (2001). Facts and figures from the worlds of e-learning, training, work, and jobs. Available from http://www.sagelearning.com/research-papers.htm

Schmoker, M. (1999). *Results: The key to continuous improvement* (2nd ed.). Alexandria, VA: ASCD.

Senge, P. (1990). *The fifth discipline: The art & practice of the learning organization.* New York: Doubleday.

Shaver, H. (2004). *Organize, communicate, empower!* Thousand Oaks, CA: Corwin.

Stack, L. (2004, May). Get home sooner. *Working Mother Magazine, 5*(27), 57–59, 86.

Timm, P. R. (1987). *Successful self-management: A psychologically sound approach to personal effectiveness.* Los Altos, CA: Crisp Publications.

Waters, T., Marzano, R., & McNulty, B. (2003). *Balanced leadership: What 30 years of research tells us about the effect of leadership on student achievement.* Aurora, CO: McREL Institute.

Weinhaus, E. (2004). *Personal survey.* Available from http://www.evonneweinhaus.com/survey.htm

Winter, M. (2004, May 13). Leave the office earlier. Available from http://www.prweb.com/releases/2004/5/prweb125473.htm

Yukl, G. (1998). *Leadership in organizations* (4th ed.). Upper Saddle River, NJ: Prentice Hall.

Index

**CORWIN
PRESS**

The Corwin Press logo—a raven striding across an open book—represents the union of courage and learning. Corwin Press is committed to improving education for all learners by publishing books and other professional development resources for those serving the field of PreK–12 education. By providing practical, hands-on materials, Corwin Press continues to carry out the promise of its motto: **"Helping Educators Do Their Work Better."**